FAIRY TALES READERS THEATRE

RECENT TITLES IN TEACHER IDEAS PRESS' READERS THEATRE SERIES

Mother Goose Readers Theatre for Beginning Readers
Anthony D. Fredericks

MORE Frantic Frogs and Other Frankly Fractured Folktales for Readers Theatre
Anthony D. Fredericks

Songs and Rhymes Readers Theatre for Beginning Readers
Anthony D. Fredericks

Readers Theatre for Middle School Boys: Investigating the Strange and Mysterious
Ann N. Black

African Legends, Myths, and Folktales for Readers Theatre
Anthony D. Fredericks

Against All Odds: Readers Theatre for Grades 3–8
Suzanne I. Barchers and Michael Ruscoe

Readers Theatre for African American History
Jeff Sanders and Nancy I. Sanders

Building Fluency with Readers Theatre: Motivational Strategies, Successful Lessons,
and Dynamic Scripts to Develop Fluency, Comprehension, Writing, and Vocabulary
Anthony D. Fredericks

American Folklore, Legends, and Tall Tales for Readers Theatre
Anthony D. Fredericks

Multi-Grade Readers Theatre: Picture Book Authors and Illustrators
Suzanne I. Barchers and Charla R. Pfeffinger

More Readers Theatre for Middle School Boys: Adventures with Mythical Creatures
Ann N. Black

Fun with Finance: Math + Literacy = Success
Written and Illustrated by Carol Peterson

FAIRY TALES
READERS THEATRE

Anthony D. Fredericks

Readers Theatre

A Teacher Ideas Press Book

Libraries Unlimited

An Imprint of ABC-CLIO, LLC

A B C • C L I O

Santa Barbara, California • Denver, Colorado • Oxford, England

Library of Congress Cataloging-in-Publication Data

Fredericks, Anthony D.
  Fairy tales readers theatre / Anthony D. Fredericks.
    p. cm.
  "A Teacher Ideas Press Book."
  Includes bibliographical references and index.
  ISBN 978-1-59158-849-8 (hard copy : alk. paper) – ISBN
  978-1-59158-851-1 (ebook) 1. Fairy tales—Study and teaching
  (Elementary) 2. Fairy tales—History and criticism. I. Title.
  LB1575.F74 2009
  372.67'6—dc22   2009017464

13   12   11   10   9   1   2   3   4   5

This book is also available on the World Wide Web as an eBook.
Visit www.abc-clio.com for details.

ABC-CLIO, LLC
130 Cremona Drive, P.O. Box 1911
Santa Barbara, California 93116-1911

This book is printed on acid-free paper ∞
Manufactured in the United States of America

Contents

Introduction vii

Part I:
Readers Theatre in the Classroom and Library

Chapter 1: Getting Started with Readers Theatre 3
Chapter 2: Performing Readers Theatre for an Audience 9

Part II:
Fairy Tales

Beauty and the Beast 17
The Elves and the Shoemaker 22
The Emperor's New Clothes 26
Hansel and Gretel 32
Jack and the Beanstalk 36
The Princess and the Pea 41
Rapunzel 44
Rumpelstiltskin 49
Snow White and the Seven Dwarfs 54
The Little Red Hen 59
The Gingerbread Man 62
Goldilocks and the Three Bears 67
Chicken Little 71
Little Red Riding Hood 77
The Three Little Pigs 81
The Ugly Duckling 85
The Three Billy Goats Gruff 90
Sleeping Beauty 94
Cinderella 99

Part III:
Fairy Tales (with a Touch of Humor)

Beauty and This Incredibly Ugly Guy 107
Coughy: The Dwarf Snow White Never Told You About 111
Don't Kiss Sleeping Beauty, She's Got Really Bad Breath 116
Goldilocks and the Three Hamsters 119
Little Red Riding Hood Punches the Wolf Character Right in the Kisser 123
The Gingerbread Boy Gets Baked at 350° for 15–20 Minutes 127

References 131
More Teacher Resources 133
Index 137

Introduction

Say the words "Once upon a time . . ." to any adult, and you will probably see a smile slip across his or her face. Those are magical words—words that conjure up stories of long ago. For most of us, they bring back pleasant memories of someone (our parents or a favorite teacher) reading (aloud) a story or book. Those words may remind us of simpler times—times long before we had to worry about home mortgages, saving for our kid's college tuition, retirement plans, or even behavioral objectives. The memories were sweet, and the recollections were always pleasurable.

Think how those same four words might affect the students with whom you work. Think of the mental journeys or creative adventures you can share with youngsters as you lead them through the magical world of children's literature. Imaginations are stimulated, and minds are filled with the delicious sounds of language in action! It is that language—the language of feeling, emotion, and passion— that excites youngsters and helps them appreciate the role literature plays in their everyday lives (as it has for generations).

And what better way to bring children's literature alive than through the magic of readers theatre? Readers theatre offers youngsters interesting and unique insights into the utility of language and its value in both its printed and oral forms. It is "language arts" in its purest form: It boosts listening and speaking skills, enhances writing abilities, powers reading development, develops positive self-concepts, and transforms reluctant readers into energized readers. Quite simply, it is literature brought to life and life brought to literature.

FAIRY TALES AND READERS THEATRE

Fairy tales have been a tradition of many cultures and countries. They are part and parcel of the human experience, because they underscore the values and experiences we cherish as well as those we seek to share with each other. Nowhere is this more important than in today's classroom or library. Perhaps it is a natural part of who we are that fairy tales command our attention and help us appreciate the values, ideas, and traditions we hold dear. So too, should students have those same experiences and those same pleasures.

Fairy tales conjure up all sorts of visions and possibilities: faraway lands, magnificent adventures, enchanted princes, beautiful princesses, evil wizards and wicked witches, a few ogres and demons, a couple of castles and cottages, perhaps a mysterious forest or two, and certainly tales of mystery, intrigue, and adventure. These are stories of tradition and timelessness, tales that enchant, mystify, and excite through a marvelous weaving of characters, settings, and plots that have stood the test of time. Our senses are stimulated, our mental images are energized, and our experiences are fortified through the magic of storytelling.

Fairy tales are also a way of sharing the power and intrigue of language. I suppose part of my belief that the sharing of fairy tales is the quintessential classroom activity lies in the fact that it is an opportunity to bring life, vitality, and substance to the two-dimensional letters and words on a printed page. So too, is it an interpersonal activity, a "never-fail" way to connect with minds and souls and hearts.

When children are provided with regular opportunities to become fairy tale storytellers, they develop a personal stake in the literature shared. They also begin to cultivate personal interpretations of that literature, which leads to higher levels of appreciation and comprehension. Practicing and performing fairy tales as readers theatre is an involvement endeavor, one that demonstrates and utilizes numerous languaging activities.

Readers theatre is a storytelling device that stimulates the imagination and promotes an appreciation for fairy tales. Simply stated, it is an oral interpretation of a piece of literature read in a dramatic style. Teachers and librarians all across the country have long promoted the powerful benefits of drama for their students: positive emotional growth, increased levels of motivation, and absolute engagement in the tasks of learning.

Simply put, readers theatre is an act of involvement, an opportunity to share, a time to creatively interact with others, and a personal interpretation of what can be or could be. It provides numerous opportunities for youngsters to make fairy tales come alive and pulsate with their own unique brand of perception and vision. In so doing, fairy tales become personal and reflective; children have a breadth of opportunities to be storytellers, just like the storytellers of long ago who created these timeless tales.

WHAT YOUR PRINCIPAL NEEDS TO KNOW

In this era of accountability and standards-based education, many educators want to know if classroom practices—whether traditional or innovative—have an impact on the literacy growth of students. Significant research on the use of readers theatre in elementary classrooms has demonstrated its positive effects on comprehension development, motivation to read, attitudes toward learning, and appreciation of reading as a lifelong skill.

What follows is a brief summary of some significant research on the impact of readers theatre on the literacy growth of students. Feel free to share this information with interested administrators, parents, or community members. Suffice it to say, readers theatre is a "research-based practice" that has been demonstrated to have a significant and powerful impact on students' reading growth and development.

❖ "Creative and critical thinking are enhanced through the utilization of readers theatre. Children are active participants in the interpretation and delivery of a story; as such, they develop thinking skills that are divergent rather than convergent, and interpretive skills that are supported rather than directed." (Fredericks 2007)

❖ "Readers theatre provides an active, analytical framework for reading and helps students to understand and interpret what they read." (Wolf 1998)

❖ "Readers theatre provides troubled readers with successful reading experiences; it can reshape images of failure into those of success and accomplishment. Readers theatre forms a bridge between troubled reading to supported reading, and ultimately, independent reading." (Dixon et al. 1996)

❖ "Readers theatre [promotes] oral reading fluency, as children [explore] and [interpret] the meaning of literature." (Martinez et al. 1999)

❖ "We are gaining evidence from classroom research that readers theatre yields improvements in students' word recognition, fluency, and comprehension." (Rasinski 2003)

❖ "[Readers theatre] is valuable for non-English speaking children or non-fluent readers. Readers theatre provides them with positive models of language usage and interpretation . . . . It allows them to see 'language in action' and the various ways in which language can be used." (Fredericks 2001)

❖ "Even resistant readers eagerly engage in practicing for readers theatre performance, reading and rereading scripts many times." (Tyler and Chard, 2000)

❖ "Second graders who did readers theatre on a regular basis made, on average, more than a year's growth in reading." (Strecker et al. 1999)

❖ "As students take on the roles of characters [in readers theatre], they also take on the roles of competent readers." (Fredericks 2008a, 2008b)

The research is clear: Classroom teachers and librarians who make readers theatre a regular and systematic component of their literacy instruction and introduction to literature will be providing those students with positive opportunities to succeed in all aspects of reading growth and development. Word recognition, vocabulary, fluency, and comprehension can all be enhanced considerably when readers theatre becomes part of the educational offerings in any classroom or library.

WHAT IS THE VALUE OF READERS THEATRE?

Above and beyond the substantive research supporting the use of readers theatre as a positive classroom and library activity, here's what I like so much about readers theatre: It allows children to breathe life and substance into literature, an interpretation that is neither right nor wrong, since it will be colored by kids' unique perspectives, experiences, and vision. The reader's interpretation of a piece of literature is intrinsically more valuable than some predetermined "translation" that might be found in a teacher's manual, for example.

Many teachers subscribe to the notion that reading involves an active and energetic relationship between the reader and the text. That is, the reader–text relationship is reciprocal and involves the characteristics of the reader as well as the nature of the material (Fredericks 2001). This philosophy of reading has particular applications for teachers and librarians building effective literacy programs. As you might expect, it also serves as a foundation for the implementation and effectiveness of readers theatre.

With that in mind, here are some of the many educational values I see in readers theatre. These have come from my own work with youngsters as a former classroom teacher and reading specialist, a thorough review of the literature on readers theatre, as well as my observations of, and conversations with, classroom teachers throughout the United States and Canada.

1. Readers theatre brings literature to life! For many students, particularly those struggling with reading, words on a page often appear as "lifeless characters"—devoid of expression, emotion, or involvement. Readers theatre, however, provides both accomplished and struggling readers with a lively and active interpretation of books. Readers get to see and participate in a personal interpretation and involvement process that "activates" the words, characters, and plots of stories.

2. Students are connected to real literature in authentic situations. They are exposed to quality literature from a wide range of authors and a wide range of genres. Many readers theatre scripts are based on real literature sources, and students can begin developing their own interpretations of literature through the creation of their own scripts based on those books. In fact, one of the best ways to help children enjoy and extend their appreciation of good books is by encouraging them to write and perform readers theatre productions after reading an appropriate piece

of literature. Readers theatre can also be used to introduce children to good literature. After performing a readers theatre script, children will be stimulated to read the original source, not to compare, but rather to extend their learning opportunities. Readers theatre may precede the reading of a related book or be used as an appropriate follow-up to the reading (oral or silent) of a good book. Quality literature and readers theatre are complementary elements of the overall literacy program that underscore children's active engagement in text.

3. Children can learn about the major features of children's literature: plot, theme, setting, point of view, and characterization. This occurs when they are provided with opportunities to design and construct their own readers theatre scripts (after experiencing prepared scripts such as those in this book or scripts that you create using books and literature shared in regular reading instruction).

4. Readers theatre helps students focus on the integration of all of the language arts: reading, writing, speaking, and listening. Children begin to see that effective communication and the comprehension of text are inexorably intertwined. Most state standards in the language arts, and all research reports about best practices in literacy, underscore literacy as an integrated series of related components. In other words, literacy growth is not just growth in reading—it is the development of reading in concert with the other language arts. The section below ("Hey, What about Standards?") provides the specific connections between each of the English/language arts standards and readers theatre. It's interesting to note how readers theatre promotes, enhances, and solidifies students' mastery of 11 of the 12 English/language arts standards (92% of the standards are enhanced with readers theatre).

5. Teachers and librarians have also discovered that readers theatre is an excellent way to enhance the development of important communication skills. Voice projection, intonation, inflection, and pronunciation skills are all promoted throughout any readers theatre production. This places more value on the processes of literacy instruction than on the products (e.g., standardized test scores).

6. Readers theatre allows children to experience stories in a supportive and nonthreatening format that underscores their active involvement. This is particularly beneficial for those students who are struggling with reading. Struggling readers often envision reading as something "done *to* a text" rather than as something "done *with* a text." This shift in perspective is often a critical factor in the success youngsters can eventually enjoy in reading. A change in attitude, a change in viewpoints, and a change in purpose often lead below-level readers to some new and interesting discoveries. Motivation, confidence, and outlook are all positively affected when students become the players and the performers. Equally important, the development and enhancement of self-concept is facilitated through readers theatre. Because children are working in concert with other children in a supportive atmosphere, their self-esteem mushrooms accordingly.

7. Readers theatre stimulates the imagination and the creation of visual images. A process of mental imagery helps readers construct "mind pictures" that serve as a way to tie together predictions, background knowledge, and textual knowledge in a satisfying experience. Once images are created, they become a permanent part of long-term memory. Just as important, they assist in the development of independent readers who are "connected" with the stories they read. It has been substantiated that when youngsters are provided with opportunities to create their own mental images, their comprehension and appreciation of a piece of writing will be enhanced considerably.

8. The central goal of reading instruction is comprehension. Comprehension is based on one's ability to make sense of printed materials. It goes beyond one's ability to remember details or recall factual information from text. Several researchers (Wiggens and McTighe 1998; Wiske 1998) suggest that students comprehend when they are able to a) connect new knowledge to their prior knowledge, b) interpret what they learn, c) apply their knowledge to new situations, and d) explain and predict events and actions. Readers theatre provides students with rich op-

portunities to accomplish all four elements of reading comprehension in a learning environment that is both supportive and engaged. Giving meaning to print is one of the major results of readers theatre, just as it is one of the major results of comprehension instruction.

9. Cunningham and Allington (2003) have shown that readers theatre is a perfect multilevel activity that allows teachers to group students heterogeneously rather than by ability, as is done in traditional reading programs. It provides teachers with varied options to group students by interest and desire rather than by reading level. Parts can be assigned that are sufficiently challenging (instructional level) without forcing students to deal with material at their frustration level of reading. Because students will have multiple opportunities to practice their "reading materials" at an appropriate level, they will be able to achieve levels of both competence and fluency not normally provided in more traditional, "round robin" reading activities.

10. Readers theatre is a participatory event. The characters as well as the audience are all intimately involved in the design, structure, and delivery of the story. Children begin to realize that reading is not a solitary activity, but rather one that can be shared and discussed with others. As a result, readers theatre enhances the development of cooperative learning strategies. Not only does readers theatre require youngsters to work together toward a common goal, but even more important, it supports their efforts in doing so.

11. Because it is the performance that drives readers theatre, children are given more opportunities to invest themselves and their personalities in the production of a readers theatre. The same story may be subject to several different presentations depending on the group or the individual youngsters involved.

12. When children are provided with opportunities to write or script their own readers theatre, their writing abilities are supported and encouraged. As children become familiar with the design and format of readers theatre scripts, they can begin to utilize their own creative talents in designing their own scripts. Readers theatre also exposes students to many examples of quality literature. That literature serves as positive models for their own writing. Just as authors of children's books write for authentic purposes (e.g., to entertain, to inform, to convince), so too will students understand the value of purposeful writing as they craft original readers theatre scripts or adaptations from popular books and stories.

13. Readers theatre is fun! Children of all ages have delighted in using readers theatre for many years. It is delightful and stimulating, encouraging and fascinating, relevant and personal. It is a classroom or library activity filled with a cornucopia of instructional possibilities and educational ventures.

"HEY, WHAT ABOUT STANDARDS?"

In response to a demand for a cohesive set of standards that address overall curriculum design and comprehensive student performance expectations in reading and language arts education, the International Reading Association, in concert with the National Council of Teachers of English, developed and promulgated the *IRA/NCTE Standards for the English Language Arts*. These standards provide a focused outline of the essential components of a well-structured language arts curriculum.

The 12 standards place an emphasis on literacy development as a lifelong process—one that starts well before youngsters enter school and continues throughout their lives. Thus, these standards are intentionally integrative and multidisciplinary. Just as important, they support and underscore the values of readers theatre (see above) as a multipurpose language arts activity—one appropriate for both classroom and library.

The chart on p. xii provides an abridged version of the *Standards for the English Language Arts*. Along with each standard (as appropriate) is how readers theatre serves as a valuable and innovative teaching tool in support of that standard.

English/Language Arts Standards*	Readers Theatre Support
1. Students are engaged in a wide variety of print and nonprint resources.	Readers theatre introduces students to a wealth of literature from a variety of literary sources.
2. Students are exposed to many genres of literature.	Readers theatre offers students a range of reading materials that span the eight basic genres of children's literature.
3. Students use many reading strategies to comprehend text.	Readers theatre invites students to assume an active role in comprehension development through their engagement and participation.
4. Students communicate in a variety of ways.	Readers theatre invites students to practice reading, writing, listening, and speaking in an enjoyable and educative process.
5. Students learn through writing.	Readers theatre encourages students to develop their own scripts and share them with a receptive audience.
6. Students use a variety of language conventions to understand text.	Readers theatre encourages students to discuss and understand how language conveys ideas.
7. Students are involved in personally meaningful research projects.	Readers theatre invites youngsters to examine and explore stories from a wide range of perspectives.
8. Students are comfortable with technology.	
9. Students gain an appreciation of language in a variety of venues.	Readers theatre encourages students to look at language and language use in a host of educational formats.
10. Non-English-speaking students develop competencies in all the language arts.	Readers theatre offers models of English use in a fun and engaging format.
11. Students are members of a host of literacy communities.	Readers theatre provides creative, investigative, and dynamic opportunities to see language in action.
12. Students use language for personal reasons.	Readers theatre offers innumerable opportunities for students to engage in personally enriching language activities.

*Modified and abridged from *Standards for the English Language Arts*, International Reading Association/National Council of Teachers of English, 1996.

When reviewing these standards, it should become evident that many can be promoted through the regular and systematic introduction of readers theatre into the elementary language arts curriculum. Equally important, those standards assist teachers and librarians in validating the impact and significance of readers theatre as a viable and valuable instructional tool—in language arts and throughout the entire elementary curriculum.

PART I

READERS THEATRE IN THE CLASSROOM AND LIBRARY

CHAPTER 1

Getting Started with Readers Theatre

INTRODUCING READERS THEATRE TO STUDENTS

Ever since I wrote my first book of readers theatre scripts—*Frantic Frogs and Other Frankly Fractured Folktales for Readers Theatre* (1993)—I have been amazed by and delighted with the incredible response readers theatre has generated among educators across the country. Teachers in urban, suburban, and rural schools have all told me of the incredible power of readers theatre as a regular feature of their language arts or reading curricula. In more than one dozen subsequent books on readers theatre (please see "More Teacher Resources by Anthony D. Fredericks" in the back of this book), I have shared (and seen) the passion and excitement that is so much a part of a curriculum infused with readers theatre.

In the teacher in-service programs I conduct and conference workshops I lead on readers theatre, I continue to receive rave reviews of readers theatre as a way of helping students take an active role in the reading process. Many teachers have commented on the improved levels of motivation and heightened participation in all aspects of the reading curriculum when readers theatre has been added to students' daily literacy activities.

However, readers theatre is not something that you just "drop into" the curriculum one day and expect students to enthusiastically embrace it. It must be introduced to students on a gradual basis —over the course of several days or several weeks—to achieve maximum impact. Of course, no two teachers will introduce readers theatre in exactly the same way. What follows is an instructional plan of action that allows for a great deal of latitude and variation depending on how your reading or language arts program is organized as well as the specific time constraints of your classroom schedule. Feel free to make any necessary adjustments or modifications in the schedule to suit your personal philosophy or the specific instructional needs of your students.

My experience, as well as that of many teachers, is that students need to transition through four stages in order for readers theatre to become a viable component of your overall literacy program. These four stages follow:

1. **Introduction.** This is the stage at which students are first introduced to readers theatre. In cases where most of the students in your class have been using readers theatre in previous grades, this stage can be eliminated.

2. **Familiarization.** In this stage students become comfortable with the concept of readers theatre. They begin to understand its value as an instructional tool as well as its worth in helping them become accomplished and fluent readers.

3. **Practice.** Here students are offered a variety of ways in which to practice readers theatre in authentic situations. Students begin to see positive growth and development in both reading fluency and comprehension.

4. **Integration.** This stage provides students with regular and systematic opportunities to use readers theatre as a significant element in other aspects of the reading program (e.g., guided reading, literature circles) as well as other subject areas (e.g., science, social studies).

What follows are some suggested instructional activities and presentations to share with your students. These suggestions are general in nature and can be easily incorporated into one or more lesson plans. Again, depending on the dynamics of your overall classroom reading program or library program, the lessons may last for as little as 10 minutes or as much as one hour.

1. **Introduction** (suggested duration: 1–3 days)

    A. Select a prepared readers theatre script. Choose one of the scripts from this book or from any other readers theatre collection of scripts. Duplicate sufficient copies of the script for every member of the class.

    B. Distribute the scripts to students. Tell students that a readers theatre script is exactly like a script used by actors and actors in television, the movies, or plays. The only difference is that in readers theatre the lines don't have to be memorized. Nevertheless, they still have to be read with the same level of enthusiasm and emotion that professional actors use.

    C. Identify and discuss the various printed elements of the script. Identify the narrator, the staging instructions, how the various actor parts are designated, any emotional suggestions noted for specific characters, and other features.

    D. Invite students to silently read through the script on their own. You may wish to use the script as part of a guided reading lesson. Afterward, ask students to share what they noted in the script (e.g., a narrator, a different style of writing, short parts and long parts). Record students' observations on the chalkboard and plan time to discuss them.

    E. Use the script as a read-aloud for your students. Tell students that you are going to model how a readers theatre script should be read. Inform them that you will also be modeling fluent and expressive reading. You will add emotion to certain parts and will maintain a consistent rate throughout the reading, as well. Invite students to listen carefully to this initial reading.

F. After reading through the script, invite students to discuss what they heard. How did your reading differ from other read-alouds in the classroom? How was it similar? What did they enjoy about your reading? How might they have presented the script? Record their observations on the chalkboard.

G. As appropriate, show students another prepared readers theatre script. Invite them to identify selected elements of the script (narrator, specific characters, staging directions, etc.). Make sure students understand that most readers theatre scripts follow a fairly standard format.

2. Familiarization (suggested duration: 1 week)

Before engaging students in this stage, you may wish to select 5 to 10 lines or passages from a forthcoming script. It is suggested that these lines or passages come from the beginning of the script and that they be representative of most (if not all) of the characters (including any narrator(s)). Record these passages on cardboard sentence strips (using block printing or a word processing program).

Here are some sample sentence strips from beginning of the readers theatre script "The Gingerbread Man") :

NARRATOR 1	Once upon a time there was a Little Old Woman . . . .

LITTLE OLD WOMAN	That's me!

NARRATOR 2	. . . and a Little Old Man.

LITTLE OLD MAN	That's me!

NARRATOR 1	Well, they both lived alone in a little old house in the middle of the little old woods. They were very lonely, so one day the Little Old Woman decided to make a Gingerbread Boy.

After creating the necessary sentence strips engage students in the following sequence of activities:

A. Select a prepared readers theatre script (one from this book, for example, or any other collection of scripts). Record the script on audiotape (you may wish to alter your voice slightly for each of the characters or enlist the aid of some other teachers, or parents, to help you record the script). Make sure this recording of the script is fluent and smooth (practice several times if necessary).

B. Provide students with copies of the selected script. Point out, once more, how a readers theatre script is organized (e.g., narrator, individual characters, etc.). Tell students that they will listen to a reading of the script on an audiotape.

C. Play the recording for students. Invite them to listen carefully for the smooth and fluent reading. Encourage them, as appropriate, to follow along by pointing to each word as they hear it.

D. You may wish to repeat the sequence above, particularly if you are using this sequence with a group of struggling readers who may need some additional reinforcement and assistance.

E. Provide an opportunity for students to discuss what they heard, the intonation exhibited by the readers, the smoothness of their delivery, or any other aspects of the recording. You may wish to record these observations on the chalkboard or a sheet of newsprint.

F. Invite the class (or group) to read through the entire script chorally. You should also participate in this choral reading so that students have a positive model and an appropriate support system for their oral reading. At this stage, it would be appropriate to emphasize the emotions that selected characters may bring to their parts (e.g., anger, disgust, happiness).

G. After the choral reading, randomly distribute the sentence strips to selected students. Inform the students that they will now become the characters in the play. Invite the students to stand in a line. Point to each character (using the sequence in the script) and invite each student to read his or her selected passage.

H. Invite other students to listen and comment (in a positive way) about the presentation of the first part of the script.

I. Distribute the sentence strips to another group of students and invite them to line up and recite the passages as the previous group did. Again, it would be appropriate to discuss the nature of the presentation in a supportive atmosphere.

J. (optional) Play the recorded version of the script again for the students. Invite them to make any additional comments.

3. **Practice** (suggested duration: 1–2 weeks)

A. Select, duplicate, and distribute a prepared script to all the students in your class. *Note:* At this particular stage I have frequently given students a selection of possible scripts from which the entire class makes a single choice. This gives students a sense of ownership over the script, which ultimately results in a heightened level of motivation.

B. Divide the class into pairs or triads of students. Invite students to share the script in their small groups. Students may wish to read the script silently, after which they may discuss the story line, characters, plot, or other elements. Students may also elect to read certain sections to each other, not only to practice fluent reading, but also to get a "feel" for the story.

C. Assign roles. I like to assign one student from each of the small groups to a character in the script. (If there are, for example, six characters, I make sure that students are initially divided into six small groups.) Each character then practices his or her part with the other members of his or her group (for example, the character reads only his or her own lines to group members, who assist with any difficult words or comment on the fluency of the reading).

D. When students have had sufficient practice, arrange them according to the staging directions for that script.

E. Invite the assigned students to read through the script just as they practiced it. Invite others students to listen to the presentation. After the script is completed, discuss how it might be improved the next time.

   F. (optional) Reassign roles to different students in the class. Divide the class into small groups and repeat the sequence as described above.

4. **Integration** (suggested duration: remainder of the school year or remainder of the unit)

   A. Select a prepared readers theatre script (one from this book or any other collection of scripts). Assign roles to selected students and distribute copies of the scripts to those students. You may wish to use two or three separate scripts—each one distributed to a different group of students in the class.

   B. Invite students to practice their assigned parts in preparation for a production later on. Students should be provided with practice time in class and should also be encouraged to practice their respective parts at home.

   C. Schedule a day and time when students will present their scripts to others in the class. This initial presentation should be kept as an in-class presentation to allay any fears students may have about presenting to an unfamiliar group of individuals. Ask students if they would like to invite their parents to attend this presentation.

   D. After presenting the initial script, invite students to select other prepared scripts for a more formal presentation.

   E. Invite students to create their own readers theatre scripts from self-selected literature in the classroom or school library. Make this process a normal part of your writing program or a basic element of a writer's workshop. After students have created their own scripts, provide them with opportunities to present them to appropriate audiences, including classrooms at a grade level above or below yours.

   F. Consider the implementation of readers theatre as a fundamental element in literature circles. After students have engaged in a discussion about a self-selected book, invite them to develop the book into a readers theatre script that can become a permanent part of the classroom library.

   G. Students may wish to use readers theatre as part of a thematic unit. According to Meinbach et al., "a thematic approach to learning combines structured, sequential, and well-organized strategies, activities, children's literature, and materials used to expand a particular concept" (2000, 10). Readers theatre has the advantage of offering youngsters a creative and dynamic way to utilize their reading abilities in a productive and engaging manner. By integrating readers theatre into thematic units, you will help students gain a deeper appreciation of the role of reading (and reading fluency) in their overall literacy development.

   H. Use prepared scripts or student-created scripts as part of your content area instruction. Readers theatre has been shown to stimulate curiosity (when used in advance of a content area unit) and promote enthusiasm (when used as part of an instructional unit), particularly when incorporated into a variety of subject areas (Fredericks 2007).

   I. Readers theatre can be effectively incorporated into guided reading activities in any classroom. The three critical and interrelated stages of guided reading (before reading, during reading, and after reading) offer you and your students unique opportunities to weave readers theatre into the overall reading curriculum. Imagine the thrill and excitement of students using a self-designed script as the reading selection in a guided reading group! Readers theatre holds the promise of helping students in a guided reading group understand and appreciate the richness of language, the ways in which to interpret that language, and how language can be a powerful vehicle for the comprehension and appreciation of various forms of literature (Fredericks 2001).

CHAPTER 2

Performing Readers Theatre for an Audience

One of the features of readers theatre I enjoy very much is the many ways in which it can become part of the classroom curriculum. Along with scores of other teachers, I've discovered that readers theatre can be a wonderful opportunity for students to become active participants in the entire learning process as well as engaged explorers of every curricular area.

Obviously readers theatre achieves its greatest potency when students have multiple opportunities to share it with others. This chapter focuses on ways you can make that experience incredibly successful.

SCRIPT PREPARATION

One of the advantages of using readers theatre in the classroom or library is the lack of extra work or preparation time necessary to get "up and running." If you use the scripts in this book, your preparation time will be minimal.

❖ After a script has been selected for presentation make sufficient copies. A copy of the script should be provided for each actor. In addition, making two or three extra copies (one for you and "replacement" copies for scripts that are accidentally damaged or lost) is also a good idea. Copies for the audience are unnecessary and are not suggested.

9

❖ Bind each script between two sheets of colored construction paper or poster board. Bound scripts tend to formalize the presentation a little and lend an air of professionalism to the actors.

❖ Highlight each character's speaking parts with different color highlighter pens. This helps youngsters track their parts without being distracted by the dialogue of others.

STARTING OUT

Introducing the concept of readers theatre to students for the first time may be as simple as sharing a script with an entire class and "walking" youngsters through the design and delivery of that script.

❖ Emphasize that a readers theatre performance does not require any memorization of the script. The interpretation and performance are what count.

❖ Read an entire script aloud, taking on the various roles. Let students know how easy and comfortable this process is.

❖ Encourage selected volunteers to read assigned parts of a sample script to the entire class. Readers should stand or sit in a circle so that other classmates can observe them.

❖ Provide opportunities for additional re-readings using other volunteers. Plan time to discuss the ease of presentation and the different interpretations offered by various readers.

❖ Allow readers an opportunity to practice their script before presenting it to an audience. Take some time to discuss voice intonation, facial gestures, body movements, and other features that could be used to enhance the presentation.

❖ Give children the opportunity to suggest their own modifications, adaptations, or interpretations of the script. They will undoubtedly be "in tune" with the interests and perceptions of their peers and can offer some distinctive and personal interpretations.

❖ Encourage students to select nonstereotypical roles in any readers theatre script. For example, boys can take on female roles and girls can take on male roles, the smallest person in the class can take on the role of a giant fire-breathing dragon (for example), or a shy student can take on the role of a boastful, bragging giant. Provide sufficient opportunities for students to expand and extend their appreciation of readers theatre through a variety of "out of character" roles.

STAGING

Staging involves the physical location of the readers as well as any necessary movements. Unlike in a more formal play, the movements are often minimal. The emphasis is more on presentation; less on action.

❖ For most presentations, readers will stand or sit on stools or chairs. The physical location of each reader has been indicated for each of the scripts in this book.

❖ If there are many characters in the presentation, it may be advantageous to have characters in the rear (upstage) standing while those in the front (downstage) are placed on stools or chairs. This ensures that the audience will both see and hear every actor.

❖ Usually all of the characters will be on stage throughout the duration of the presentation. For most presentations it is not necessary to have characters enter and exit. If you place the characters on stools, they may face the audience when they are involved in a particular scene and then turn around whenever they are not involved in a scene.

❖ Make simple, hand-lettered signs with the name of each character. Loop a piece of string or yarn through each sign and hang it around the neck of each respective character. That way, the audience will know the identity of each character throughout the presentation.

❖ Each reader will have her or his own copy of the script in a paper cover (see above). If possible, use a music stand for each reader's script (this allows readers to use their hands for dramatic interpretations as necessary).

❖ Several presentations have a narrator to set up the story. The narrator serves to establish the place and time of the story for the audience so that the characters can "jump into" their parts from the beginning of the story. Typically, the narrator is separated from the other "actors" and can be identified by a simple sign.

PROPS

Two positive features of readers theatre are its ease of preparation and its ease of presentation. Informality is a hallmark of any readers theatre script.

❖ Much of the setting for a story should take place in the audience's mind. Elaborate scenery is not necessary; simple props are often the best. For example:

 – A branch or potted plant may serve as a tree.

 – A drawing on the chalkboard may illustrate a building.

 – A hand-lettered sign may designate one part of the staging area as a particular scene (e.g., swamp, castle, field, forest).

 – Children's toys may be used for uncomplicated props (e.g., a telephone, vehicles).

 – A sheet of aluminum foil or a remnant of blue cloth may be used to simulate a lake or pond.

❖ Costumes for the actors are unnecessary. A few simple items may be suggested by students. For example:

 – Hats, scarves, or aprons may be used by major characters.

 – A paper cutout may serve as a tie, button, or badge.

 – Old clothing (borrowed from parents) may be used as warranted.

❖ Some teachers and librarians have discovered that the addition of appropriate background music or sound effects enhances a readers theatre presentation.

❖ It's important to remember that the emphasis in readers theatre is on the reading, not on any accompanying "features." The best presentations are often the simplest.

DELIVERY

I've often found it useful to let students know that the only difference between a readers theatre presentation and a movie role is that they will have a script in their hands. This allows them to focus more on presenting a script rather than memorizing it.

❖ When first introduced to readers theatre, students often have a tendency to "read into" their scripts. Encourage students to look up from their scripts and interact with other characters or the audience as appropriate.

❖ Practicing the script beforehand can eliminate the problem of students burying their heads in the pages. Children understand the need to involve the audience as much as possible in the development of the story.

❖ Voice projection and delivery are important in allowing the audience to understand character actions. The proper mood and intent need to be established, which is possible when children are familiar and comfortable with each character's "style."

❖ Again, the emphasis is on delivery, so be sure to suggest different types of voice (i.e., angry, irritated, calm, frustrated, excited, etc.) that children may wish to use for their particular character(s).

SCRIPT SELECTION

One of the best presentation options is when several groups of students in your classroom come together to present a selection of readers theatre scripts for an audience of enthusiastic students (from the same or a different grade) and some very appreciative parents. Here are some possibilities for you to consider:

❖ When possible, invite students to select a variety of scripts to be included in the presentation. Inform them that a combination of short scripts and longer scripts adds variety to the program. When students are invited to be part of the selection process a sense of "ownership" develops which contributes to the ultimate success of the overall presentation(s).

❖ Consider the age and grade of the audience. For younger students (grades K–2) the total program should be no longer than 20 minutes (a mix of two to four scripts). For older students (grades 3–6) the total program should be no longer than 45 minutes (a mix of five to seven scripts).

❖ If feasible, include a section of the program (parts of a script or an entire production) in which the audience takes an active role. This could include singing, clapping, repeating selected lines in a production (provide cue cards), or some other physical contribution. This would be particularly appropriate for younger audiences, whose attention span is typically short and sporadic.

"IT'S SHOW TIME!"

After scripts have been prepared or selected by you and your students, it's time to consider how, when, and where you would like to present them. There are many options to consider. The following list, which is not all-inclusive, presents a variety of presentation options for readers theatre. How you and your students present readers theatre will ultimately be determined by the nature of your overall language arts program, the time and facilities available, the comfort level of students, and the demands of your overall curriculum. You will discover that there is an almost inexhaustible array of options available.

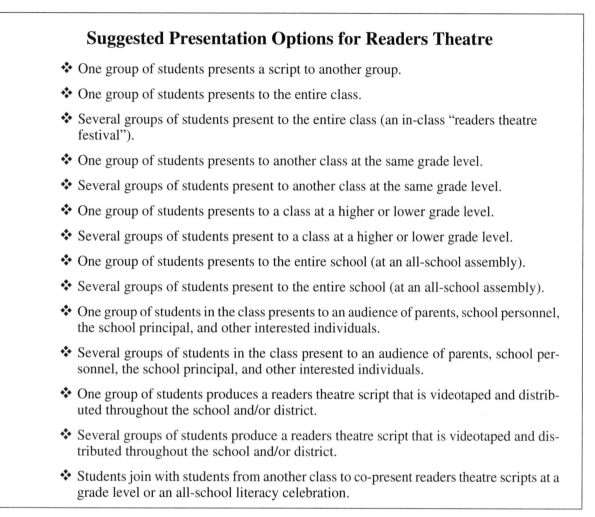

Suggested Presentation Options for Readers Theatre

❖ One group of students presents a script to another group.

❖ One group of students presents to the entire class.

❖ Several groups of students present to the entire class (an in-class "readers theatre festival").

❖ One group of students presents to another class at the same grade level.

❖ Several groups of students present to another class at the same grade level.

❖ One group of students presents to a class at a higher or lower grade level.

❖ Several groups of students present to a class at a higher or lower grade level.

❖ One group of students presents to the entire school (at an all-school assembly).

❖ Several groups of students present to the entire school (at an all-school assembly).

❖ One group of students in the class presents to an audience of parents, school personnel, the school principal, and other interested individuals.

❖ Several groups of students in the class present to an audience of parents, school personnel, the school principal, and other interested individuals.

❖ One group of students produces a readers theatre script that is videotaped and distributed throughout the school and/or district.

❖ Several groups of students produce a readers theatre script that is videotaped and distributed throughout the school and/or district.

❖ Students join with students from another class to co-present readers theatre scripts at a grade level or an all-school literacy celebration.

Suffice it to say, there is an infinite variety of presentation modes you and your students can select. It is important to share some of these options with your students and invite them to identify those with which they would be most comfortable. My rule of thumb is to "start small" at first—for example, have one or two groups of students present to the class as part of a regularly scheduled readers theatre presentation time (once a month, for example). As students gain confidence and self-assurance, they should be encouraged to take their presentations "on the road," sharing them with other classes and other grades.

INVITING AN AUDIENCE

An audience gives readers theatre legitimacy—it is a signal to students that all their hard work and practice has a purpose: to share the fruits of their labors (and their concomitant improvements in reading fluency) with an appreciative group of individuals.

❖ Consider sending announcements or invitations to parents and other interested individuals. You may wish to design these yourself or, better yet, invite students to design, illustrate, and produce the invitations.

❖ In addition to parents, I have always found it appropriate (and exciting) to invite other adults with whom the students are familiar, including, for example, the school secretary, the custodian, a bus driver or two, cafeteria workers, and aides. After the presentation the students are sure to get a raft of positive comments and lots of appreciation from these individuals as they encounter them throughout the school.

❖ As appropriate, invite community members to be part of the audience. Residents of a local senior citizen center or retirement home are a most logical (and very enthusiastic) audience. These folks are always appreciative of the work of children and are often eager to see what is happening in the local schools.

POST-PRESENTATION

As a wise author once said, "The play's the thing." So it is with readers theatre. In other words, the mere act of presenting a readers theatre script is complete in and of itself. It is not necessary, or even required, to do any type of formalized evaluation after readers theatre. Once again, the emphasis is on informality. Readers theatre can and should be a pleasurable and stimulating experience for children.

Following are a few ideas you may want to share with students. In doing so, you will be providing youngsters with important learning opportunities that extend and promote all aspects of your reading and language arts program.

❖ After a presentation, discuss with students how the script enhanced or altered the original story.

❖ Invite students to suggest other characters who could be added to the script.

❖ Invite students to suggest alternate dialogue for various characters.

❖ Invite students to suggest different setting(s) for the script.

❖ Invite students to talk about their reactions to various characters' expressions, tone of voice, presentations, or dialogues.

❖ After a presentation, invite youngsters to suggest any modifications they think could be made to the script.

PART II

FAIRY TALES

Beauty and the Beast

STAGING: The three major characters should all be placed in the front of the staging area. They may be seated in front of music stands or may each stand behind a lectern. The two narrators should be in the back and to the sides of the staging area.

Narrator 1 X			Narrator 2 X
	Father X	Beauty X	Beast X

NARRATOR 1: One upon a time there was a poor merchant who set off for market one day. Before leaving he asked each of his three daughters what she would like as a present upon his return.

NARRATOR 2: The first daughter wanted a beautiful dress. The second daughter desired a pearl necklace. But the third and youngest daughter, whose name was Beauty, said:

BEAUTY: All I would like is a rose that you have picked especially for me.

From *Fairy Tales Readers Theatre* by Anthony D. Fredericks. Santa Barbara, CA: Libraries Unlimited. Copyright © 2009.

NARRATOR 1: Soon after the merchant had completed his business in the marketplace, he set off for home. Along the way a terrible storm blew up, with great thunder, howling winds, and driving rain.

NARRATOR 2: The merchant was getting cold and wet and hoped that he could find a place to stay for the night. Suddenly he noticed a bright light in the distance, and as he drew nearer he saw a castle beside the river.

FATHER: I hope that this will be a good place to get out of the storm and take shelter for the night.

NARRATOR 1: As he walked in the open door he saw that the castle was empty. There was nobody there to greet him. And on a table in the main hall there was a splendid dinner, steaming hot, waiting for him.

NARRATOR 2: The merchant sat down and had himself a fine meal. Afterward he ventured upstairs and came upon a room with a roaring fire and a very soft bed all made up. He was very tired, so he lay down and fell fast asleep.

NARRATOR 1: The next morning when he awoke, he found a fine breakfast all laid out in an adjoining room. Upon finishing the breakfast he went out into the garden, where he had left his horse the night before.

NARRATOR 2: As he was walking through the garden, a large rose bush caught his eye. Remembering his promise to his daughter Beauty, he bent down to pick one of the roses.

NARRATOR 1: In an instant there sprang up a horrible beast, wearing very fine clothes. His two eyes were bloodshot, his voice was angry, and his words were loud.

BEAST: [angrily] You are an ungrateful man. Last night I gave you a meal and a fine bed to sleep in. And, now, all the thanks I get is the theft of my favorite flowers. I shall put you to death for your actions.

18

FATHER: Please forgive me. Do not kill me. I shall do whatever you ask. This rose was not for me, but for my daughter, Beauty. I had promised to bring her one at the end of my journey.

BEAST: I will spare your life, but only on one condition. You must bring me your daughter.

FATHER: [trembling] It shall be as you wish.

NARRATOR 2: The merchant hurried home and told his three daughters of his terrible and dreadful adventure—especially his promise to the beast.

BEAUTY: Dear father, do not worry. I will do anything for you. You will be able to keep your promise and keep your life. Take me to the castle. I will stay there, as you did promise.

FATHER: Thank you, my pretty daughter. Thank you for saving my life.

NARRATOR 1: And, so, the father took Beauty to the castle.

NARRATOR 2: However, instead of a very menacing creature, the Beast presented Beauty with a calm and polite disposition. He was very pleasant and very polite.

NARRATOR 1: In the beginning, Beauty was quite frightened of the Beast. However, in spite of the Beast's ugliness, her initial horror of him gradually faded away.

NARRATOR 2: She was given one of the finest rooms in the castle and would sit for hour upon hour embroidering in front of a roaring fire. Nearby sat the Beast, who silently watched her. They had many gentle conversations and soon became close friends. Then one day, the Beast asked her:

BEAST: I would like you to be my wife.

NARRATOR 1: Beauty was taken by surprise and did not know how to answer. He was, after all, quite ugly, but she did not want to hurt the feelings of this creature who had been so kind to her. Besides, it was this Beast who had spared her father's life.

BEAUTY: [nervously] I really don't know what to say. I so much would like to, but . . . .

BEAST: I quite understand. I am not offended by your refusal.

NARRATOR 2: Their relationship went on as before, and nothing further was said about the proposal. One day the Beast presented Beauty with a glorious magic mirror.

NARRATOR 1: When Beauty looked into the magic mirror, she could see her family, far away. She would stare for hours into the mirror, worrying about her family.

NARRATOR 2: One day the Beast came upon her and she was crying.

BEAST: What's wrong, fair Beauty?

BEAUTY: My father is very ill and very close to dying. I wish that I could see him again before he passes away.

BEAST: You are so sad, my Beauty. Go, go and see your father. But you must swear that you will return here in seven days. If you don't, then I will come and visit your father.

BEAUTY: You are so kind. You have made me very happy.

NARRATOR 1: Beauty rushed home—into the waiting arms of her father. She stayed with him, cared for him, and nursed him back to health.

NARRATOR 2: She would often talk about how kind the Beast was, the gentle conversations they would have by the roaring fire, and the many quiet times they had together.

NARRATOR 1: The days went by, and Beauty's father was finally nursed back to full health. Beauty was happy at last. But unfortunately she had failed to notice that the seven days had gone by.

NARRATOR 2: One night she awoke from a strange dream— actually a terrible nightmare. She had dreamt that the Beast was dying and was calling for her. He was in great agony and wanted her by his side.

NARRATOR 1: She knew she must leave at once. Grabbing her favorite horse, she rode as fast as she could back to the castle. When she arrived, she rushed up the stairs, calling his name.

NARRATOR 2: She looked in every room, but he was nowhere to be found. She rushed out into the garden and there, lying in the garden as though dead, was the Beast. She threw herself on him and hugged him tightly.

BEAUTY: [pleading] Don't die! Please don't die! I will marry you! Yes, I will marry you!

NARRATOR 1: At those words a miracle took place. The Beast's ugliness turned into the features of a very handsome prince.

BEAST: How I have waited for this moment! Many years ago an evil witch cast a spell on me and turned me into a monster. I was told that only the love of a beautiful maiden could break the spell. And at last, you have done it. My fair Beauty, I would be so happy if you'll now marry me.

NARRATOR 2: And so it was that their wedding took place in the garden of the castle. And every day after that the young prince would give his Beauty a fresh new rose. And even unto this day, the castle is known as the Castle of the Roses.

The Elves and the Shoemaker

STAGING: There are no characters in this script, just four narrators. Each of the narrators should be seated on a tall stool or chair. Each narrator's script should be placed on an individual music stand.

Narrator 1	Narrator 2	Narrator 3	Narrator 4
X	X	X	X

NARRATOR 1: In a time long ago there lived a shoemaker. Every day he worked very hard. And he was always honest with all his customers.

NARRATOR 2: Making a living as a shoemaker was very difficult, and even though the shoemaker worked and worked, he always had less and less.

NARRATOR 3: Finally, one day he found that everything he had was gone—save for just enough leather to make a single pair of shoes.

NARRATOR 4: And so he cut the leather out—making it ready for work the next day. It was his intention to rise early the next morning and craft the finest pair of shoes he could. And so that evening he went to bed and fell fast asleep.

NARRATOR 1: The next morning the shoemaker awoke with the sun in his eyes. He washed his face and prepared himself a fine, though meager, breakfast. Then, when he went to his bench to begin work on the leather, he discovered a great surprise.

NARRATOR 2: There stood the shoes, all ready made, on the table. The old shoemaker did not know what to say or what to think. This was truly an odd happening.

NARRATOR 3: The shoemaker looked carefully at the pair of shoes on the table. They were of fine workmanship—there was not a bad stitch anywhere to be found. This was a pair of shoes all neat and trim.

NARRATOR 4: That they were of excellent workmanship there was no question. They were, in all respects, a fine, fine masterpiece.

NARRATOR 1: Later that morning a customer came into the shop. He immediately saw the fine pair of shoes and offered the shoemaker a fine price for them—a price that was much higher than he would have normally charged.

NARRATOR 2: The poor shoemaker was overjoyed. He promptly purchased enough leather to make two pairs of shoes.

NARRATOR 3: That evening he cut out all his work and laid the leather pieces on the workbench so that he could begin sewing the two pairs of shoes in the morning.

NARRATOR 4: It was with a happy heart that he went to bed early. When he awoke the next morning, he rushed into his workroom and there, on the table, were two pairs of the finest shoes all sewn and expertly pieced. The shoemaker was overcome with joy.

NARRATOR 1: Soon buyers came into the store—each of whom paid the shoemaker handsomely for the fine shoes. Again, much more than he would have previously charged.

NARRATOR 2: And so, once again flush with coins, the old shoemaker purchased enough leather for four pairs of shoes.

NARRATOR 3: As before, he cut out the strips, laid them carefully on the workbench, and went gladly off to bed. The following morning, as before, there were fine shoes all neatly stitched waiting on the table. And, as before, they all commanded a fine price.

NARRATOR 4: Again and again the cycle repeated. More shoes, more leather, and more money came to the old shoemaker. He was making a fine living for himself and his wife.

NARRATOR 1: One late winter's day, around Christmastime, the old shoemaker and his wife were sitting by the fireplace chatting about the weather and other things.

NARRATOR 2: The old shoemaker turned to his wife and said that he would like to sit up that night just to see who it was that came and crafted such fines shoes every evening.

NARRATOR 3: The shoemaker's wife thought that was a fine idea and readily agreed to it.

NARRATOR 4: The old shoemaker and his wife left a small light burning and then hid themselves in a closet beside the workroom. They waited and they watched.

NARRATOR 1: In the distance they heard the tolling of the church bell—midnight had come. And, just like that—as quick as a wink—in danced two tiny dwarfs. Neither of them had a stitch of clothing on.

NARRATOR 2: The two naked dwarfs sat themselves down at the workbench. They gathered up the tools and the strips of leather and began to craft their shoes.

NARRATOR 3: The old shoemaker and his wife could not believe their eyes. The two dwarfs stitched and tapped and rapped with great care. They crafted fine, fine shoes— indeed, the finest the shoemaker had ever seen.

NARRATOR 4: The two dwarfs worked all through the night. Just before daybreak they laid out all their products on the table and, with a twinkle in their eyes, hurried away as quick as lightning.

NARRATOR 1: The next day the wife told the shoemaker that the two little dwarfs were responsible for their newfound riches. They were, she said, the reason for their good fortune. However, she felt sorry for the fact that they had no clothes on their backs and suggested that they both work at making tiny shirts and coats and waistcoats and pants. And, of course, tiny shoes.

NARRATOR 2: The thought pleased the old shoemaker very much, so he and his wife worked all day to craft the tiny clothes for their two midnight visitors.

NARRATOR 3: That evening the old shoemaker and his wife, finished and satisfied with their task, laid the tiny clothes on the table.

NARRATOR 4: As before, the shoemaker and his wife hid in a nearby closet and waited patiently for their two midnight friends.

NARRATOR 1: About midnight, the two little dwarfs danced and skipped and hopped into the room.

NARRATOR 2: As they jumped up on the table, they saw the two tiny sets of clothes before them. Filled with mirth and laughter, they dressed themselves in the twinkling of an eye.

NARRATOR 3: Once again, they danced and capered about the room. They were as merry as could be. Finally they danced their way out the door and over the village green.

NARRATOR 4: The shoemaker and his wife never saw their two tiny friends again. But their lives and their fortunes were good, and they lived in prosperity for a very long time.

The Emperor's New Clothes

STAGING: The characters should all be seated on tall stools or chairs. Place a music stand in front of each character. You may wish to use a towel as a robe or regal cape for the emperor.

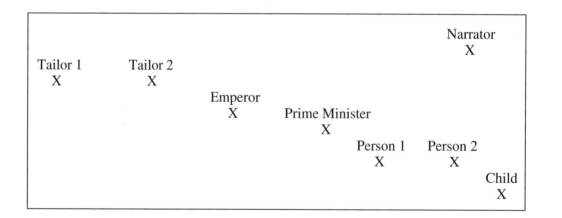

NARRATOR: Once upon a time there lived a very selfish and vain ruler—an emperor whose only thought in life was to be dressed in the finest clothes in the kingdom. He had room upon room full of clothes, and he liked nothing better than to change his clothes constantly every day and show them off to everyone he could.

 From *Fairy Tales Readers Theatre* by Anthony D. Fredericks. Santa Barbara, CA: Libraries Unlimited. Copyright © 2009.

Well, as is often the case in these old tales, there were two dishonest men who had heard of the ruler's desire to have only the finest clothes and be seen in those clothes as often as possible. So, being the scoundrels they were, they decided to hatch a plan to fool the king once and for all. They journeyed to the gates of the palace and introduced themselves to the guards.

TAILOR 1: We are two fine tailors—indeed, we are the finest in all the land.

TAILOR 2: Yes. And after many years of hard work and research, we have invented an extraordinary method of weaving a cloth that is so fine and light that it looks invisible.

TAILOR 1: Yes, indeed. As a matter of fact, this fine cloth is invisible to anyone who is too stupid and incompetent to appreciate its quality.

NARRATOR: The guards immediately summoned the prime minister. The prime minister ran to the chambers of the emperor, who was changing his clothes, to tell him the news.

PRIME MINISTER: Your Highness! Word has reached me that there are two tailors who wish to meet with you. They say that they have a magical cloth—a fine cloth—that is so light and so fine that it is invisible.

EMPEROR: Then send them to me. I wish to see this fine and invisible cloth.

NARRATOR: The two scoundrels were summoned and appeared before the emperor.

TAILOR 1: Your Highness, besides being invisible, this fine cloth can be woven in colors and patterns created especially for only you.

TAILOR 2: Yes, Your Excellency. You shall be the only one in the kingdom to have such cloth as this. We should like to begin working on this immediately.

NARRATOR: The emperor gave the two men a large bag of gold coins in exchange for their promise to begin working on the fine fabric immediately. The two scoundrels gathered together an old loom, some scraps of fabric, pieces of silk, and some gold thread. They pretended to work on the magic fabric.

The emperor thought that he had gotten a fine deal in the bargain. Not only would he be getting an extraordinary suit, he would be able to determine which of the people in his kingdom was ignorant or incompetent. So, after a few days the emperor called his prime minister.

EMPEROR: Go and see how the work on the magical fabric is proceeding. I wish to know right away.

NARRATOR: The prime minister went to the room where the two tailors were working . . . or pretending to work.

PRIME MINISTER: How is your work proceeding, my friends?

TAILOR 1: We are very close to being finished. We need some more gold thread, but we shall soon be finished.

TAILOR 2: Yes, come and feel the softness of this fabric. Come and see its bright colors. As a wise and intelligent man, you will surely appreciate this fine, fine fabric.

NARRATOR: The prime minister moved close to the loom and tried to see the fabric that was not there. He was very nervous. He thought to himself that if he couldn't see anything, that would mean that he was stupid or even incompetent. He could never admit it, because that would mean an instant dismissal from his office. So he thought quickly.

PRIME MINISTER: This is, indeed, a marvelous fabric. It is the finest I have ever seen! I must tell the emperor. He, too, will be most impressed.

NARRATOR: The two scoundrels were pleased. Their plan was working and would be ready to spring in a very short time.

Two days later the two tailors sent word that they would like to see the emperor so that they could take the necessary measurements for the new suit. The two tailors entered the royal chamber, pretending to be holding a large roll of the magic fabric.

TAILOR 1: Here is the magical fabric, Your Highness. We have worked long and hard and are honored to present this incredible fabric to you at this time.

TAILOR 2: Look at the colors and feel how fine this is. This is truly the finest fabric in all the land. Come, look!

NARRATOR: Of course the emperor could not feel the fabric, nor could he see any colors. He was in a state of panic. What should he do? What should he say? But then he realized that nobody would know that he could not see the fabric. Suddenly he felt a little better, knowing that nobody could discover that he was incompetent or stupid. And of course the emperor didn't know that everyone else in the room was thinking the same thing.

This was just what the two tailors wanted to happen. After taking the emperor's measurements, the two of them began to cut the air with scissors and began to sew with invisible thread. Finally they announced that they had completed the emperor's new suit.

TAILOR 1: Your Highness, you will have to take off your clothes in order to try on this new suit.

TAILOR 2: Yes, Your Excellency, we must see how this new suit looks on you.

NARRATOR: The emperor removed all of his clothes. The two tailors pretended to drape him with the new suit. After a few minutes they held up a mirror so that the emperor could admire himself. Nobody said anything for fear of being thought stupid or incompetent.

EMPEROR: Yes, yes. This is a very fine suit. It looks excellent. You have done a very fine job with this suit.

PRIME MINISTER: Your Highness, there is a request for you. The people of your kingdom have learned about this fine new suit of yours. They are eager to see you in your new suit.

NARRATOR: The emperor was worried about appearing in front of all those people naked. But then he thought to himself that he really wasn't naked—he was wearing a fine and excellent new suit. A suit that could obviously be seen my all, except those who were stupid or incompetent.

EMPEROR: Very well. I will grant the people the privilege of seeing me in my new suit.

NARRATOR: And so a grand parade was formed. The emperor, very naked, but thinking that he was clothed in a fine, new suit, led the parade down the middle of the road. People from near and far crowded the parade route to see the emperor's new clothes. Everyone pushed closer to get a good look.

Grand applause welcomed the procession. Of course, everyone wanted to know how stupid or incompetent his or her neighbor was. But as the emperor passed by, there was a strange murmur going through the crowd.

PERSON 1: What a fine set of clothes!

PERSON 2: What a grand new suit!

PERSON 1: Look at the emperor's new clothes. They are beautiful!

PERSON 2: They are the finest in all the land!

NARRATOR: All the people pretended that they did, indeed, see a beautiful new set of clothes on the emperor. Of course, to do otherwise would be to admit that one was stupid or incompetent. And nobody was willing to admit to his or her stupidity.

As the procession moved down the road, it moved past a young child who had not been told about the emperor's new clothes.

CHILD: The emperor is naked! Look, the emperor is naked!

PERSON 1: You don't know what you're talking about!

CHILD: Look for yourself. The emperor doesn't have a stitch of clothing on.

PERSON 2: He's right. Look, the emperor is naked. It's true—he is not wearing a thing!

NARRATOR: Finally, the emperor realized that he wasn't wearing a fine new set of clothes, but that he was, indeed, naked. He also realized that the only stupid and incompetent person in the kingdom was himself. He had been fooled . . . and fooled quite well!

Hansel and Gretel

STAGING: One narrator may stand at a lectern or podium on each side of the staging area. The father, Hansel, and Gretel may walk across the staging area during various parts of the performance. Place a cardboard box in front of the witch to serve as a make-shift oven.

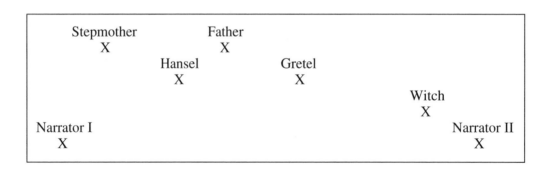

NARRATOR I: Once upon a time there lived a poor woodcutter, his two children—Hansel and Gretel—and his second wife, a very mean stepmother.

NARRATOR II: The stepmother was always nagging the woodcutter.

STEPMOTHER: There is never enough food in this house for all of us. There are too many mouths to feed. You must get rid of the two brats so that we may survive. Take them away. Take them far, far away so that they will never find their way back. You must get rid of them.

NARRATOR I: The woodcutter didn't know what to do. But he didn't want to upset his new wife.

NARRATOR II: Hansel had overheard the conversation. Thinking quickly he went into the kitchen and took a small loaf of bread and put it under his coat.

STEPMOTHER: Get rid of them, I say. You must take them away, old man. We cannot feed them, we cannot feed them. They are far too much bother.

WOODCUTTER: All right, wife. I will take them away. I will take them far into the forest and leave them there to survive on their own.

NARRATOR I: At dawn the next day, the woodcutter led Hansel and Gretel into the forest. Clever Hansel, however, walked behind his father. Every so often he would drop a small morsel of bread on the trail behind them.

HANSEL: Do not be afraid, my sister. We shall find our way back to the cottage. All we have to do is follow the trail of breadcrumbs I've left along the trail.

GRETEL: Are you sure this will work, dear brother?

HANSEL: Trust me, it will work. We shall find our way home.

NARRATOR II: The woodcutter led his children deeper and deeper into the woods. Finally, when the woods were very dark with large trees, he turned and spoke to his children.

WOODCUTTER: I am sorry, my children, but I must leave you here. There is not enough food at home to feed all of us. Be good and take care of each other.

GRETEL: Father, we are scared.

WOODCUTTER: I know, my child. But you have your brother to care for you.

NARRATOR I: And with that the woodcutter turned around and went back home.

HANSEL: Do not be afraid, dear sister. Remember, I have left a trail of bread crumbs along the way. All we need do is follow the crumbs, and we shall be home in no time.

NARRATOR II: But the little boy had forgotten about the hungry birds that lived in the forest. When they saw him dropping the crumbs, they flew along behind, and in no time at all had eaten all the crumbs. When the children tried to find their way back along the trail, they saw to their horror that all the crumbs had gone.

GRETEL: I'm scared, dear brother. I'm cold and I'm hungry, and I want to go back home.

HANSEL: Don't be afraid. I'll look after you.

NARRATOR I: The two children, scared and hungry, huddled together under a large tree. They soon fell asleep, and when dawn broke the next morning, they started to wander through the forest. They knew they were lost, but still they walked on. Suddenly they came upon a small cottage in the middle of a small meadow.

GRETEL: Look, Hansel, this cottage is made of candy.

HANSEL: Yes, the walls are made of chocolate. The roof is icing. The fence posts are candy canes. The path is made of lemon drops.

NARRATOR II: The children, who were very hungry, began to eat pieces of the house. They had never tasted anything so delicious. Everything was good—good and sweet.

NARRATOR I: Suddenly, they heard a voice.

WITCH: [sounding evil] Well, well, what do we have here? I see two little children who have fallen into my trap. They shall make a delicious dinner.

NARRATOR II: The witch took the two children into her cottage and locked them both in a cage.

34

WITCH: You two are nothing but skin and bones. I should like to have you for dinner, but I must fatten you up a bit.

NARRATOR I: For days she fed the two children loaves of bread and fat chickens. Finally she could wait no longer.

WITCH: I think you both are ready for dinner—my dinner. I shall light the stove and prepare my meal—my meal of two very plump children. Now, I'll take you out of your cages while I test the oven.

NARRATOR II: Hansel and Gretel stood beside the witch as she stuck her head inside the oven to see if it was hot enough. Gretel gave her a tremendous shove, and Hansel slammed the oven door shut.

WITCH: Help, help! Let me out! Let me out!

NARRATOR I: But the two children put a padlock on the oven door. In very short order the witch was burnt to a crisp.

GRETEL: We must find our way home, dear brother.

HANSEL: Yes, let's take this basket and fill it with food and find a trail that will lead us home.

NARRATOR II: But when the children took the basket down from the shelf, they saw that it was filled with gold coins. They were overcome with joy and gladness. They quickly set off through the woods in search of their home.

NARRATOR I: Luck was with them, for on the second day they saw their father coming toward them.

WOODCUTTER: Children, children. Your stepmother is dead. Come home with me now. I have found you, and we shall be together again.

GRETEL: Promise that you will never leave us alone again.

WOODCUTTER: I promise.

HANSEL: Look, father. We are rich! We have a basket full of gold coins. We shall never be hungry again.

NARRATOR II: And it came to pass that they all lived happily together ever after.

Jack and the Beanstalk

STAGING: The narrator should be positioned behind a lectern or at a music stand. The other characters may have their scripts in their hands and walk around the staging area as they say their lines.

```
Narrator
X
                                                          Man
                                                          X
         Mother        Jack
         X             X
                            Giant         Wife
                            X             X
```

NARRATOR: Once, in a long ago time, there lived a widow and her son, Jack. They were very poor—so poor that they often did not have enough to eat. Now Jack was a lazy boy, who never liked to work—which made matters even worse. Finally there came a day when they had to sell their cow to get money for food. With tears in her eyes the poor woman told Jack to take the cow to the market and get the best price he could for it. Jack tied a rope around the cow's neck and set off down the road. In short order he met a man on the road.

MAN: That is a fine cow. Are you taking it to market?

JACK: Yes, I am.

MAN: That is a fine cow. I would like to buy the cow from you. I have some very magic beans here, and I will exchange these magic beans for your fine cow.

NARRATOR: Jack could not resist the offer from the man. However, when he got home and told his mother what he had done, she burst into tears.

MOTHER: Jack, Jack, you silly, silly boy. What have you done? You've traded our cow for a bunch of beans.

NARRATOR: And with that, she threw the beans out the window and sent Jack off to bed without his supper. However, the next morning, when Jack looked out his window, he saw a most wonderful sight. The beans had taken root in the garden and the great stalks had grown up, higher than the clouds, forming an enormous ladder into the sky.

Filled with curiosity, Jack climbed the beanstalk, higher and higher, until he found himself in a very strange country. Looking around, he saw a castle in the distance and began to walk toward it. He walked up to the very large door and pounded his fist on it. A very tall woman opened the door.

WIFE: What do you want?

JACK: I am hungry and tired. Can you give me some bread and a place to lay my head for the night?

WIFE: Don't you know that my husband is a giant ogre who would rather eat little boys like yourself than do anything else? Your life will be in great danger if you stay here. You must go away.

NARRATOR: Jack persisted. Finally the giant's wife, who had a kind heart, decided to let him in. She led him to the kitchen and gave him some hot soup and a crust of bread. Jack had barely begun to eat when there came a frightful noise.

WIFE: Quick, it is my husband, and he is not in a good mood. Here, hide in the oven.

NARRATOR: Jack quickly scrambled inside the oven just as the giant entered the kitchen.

GIANT: Fee Fi Fo Fum!
I smell the blood of an Englishman!
Be he alive or be he dead,
I'll grind his bones to make my bread!

WIFE: Do not be concerned, my husband. What you smell is just the roast left over from last night.

NARRATOR: The giant grumbled, but he sat down beside the fire and began to eat his supper. Jack watched him carefully from inside the oven. Finally, the giant finished his meal.

GIANT: Wife, fetch me my bags of gold. I want to count my coins.

NARRATOR: With that, the wife went to a large cupboard and got down three very heavy bags of gold coins. She dumped the shiny coins onto the table, whereupon the giant scooped them into large piles and began to count them. Before long he fell fast asleep. In no time, Jack crept out of the oven, snatched one of the bags, and ran out of the house and down the road to the top of the beanstalk. He quickly climbed down the beanstalk and ran to his mother in the house.

JACK: Look, mother, we have all the money we need. We shall never be hungry again.

MOTHER: Jack, you are wonderful!

38

NARRATOR: His mother was overcome with happiness. She called Jack the best son in the world. They both lived very well for quite some time with all the things they could buy with the money.

But there came a day when there were only a few coins left. Jack decided to climb back up the beanstalk once again and visit the giant's castle. He walked down the road and up to the castle door. Someone had left the castle door ajar, so Jack slipped inside the castle and entered the kitchen.

Soon he heard the giant come home for supper. As soon as the giant entered the house, he began to roar.

GIANT: Fee Fi Fo Fum!
I smell the blood of an Englishman!
Be he alive or be he dead,
I'll grind his bones to make my bread!

WIFE: You do not smell anything, my husband. That is just a squirrel who has fallen down the chimney.

NARRATOR: The giant grumbled, but in time he sat down to consume a whole roast pig and an enormous goblet of wine. Wiping his mouth on his sleeve, he called to his wife.

GIANT: Wife, get me my golden hen. I want my golden hen.

WIFE: As you wish, my husband.

NARRATOR: The wife went and fetched the golden hen and set it down on the table. From the oven, Jack watched as the golden hen laid an egg of solid gold. He could not believe his eyes—a hen that laid golden eggs!

Jack waited. Soon, just as before, the giant began to nod, and before long he fell fast asleep. Jack slowly snuck out of the oven, seized the golden hen, and ran to the door. Just before he got out the door the golden hen cackled. The noise woke up the giant, and he began to roar.

GIANT: [loudly] Who is stealing my golden hen? WHO IS STEALING MY GOLDEN HEN? I shall grab him and eat him in one bite.

NARRATOR: Jack was so frightened that he ran with all his speed. However, the giant, with his large steps, began to catch up to Jack. Jack could feel the giant's breath like a hot wind on his back.

Jack reached the top of the beanstalk and clambered down as fast as he could. The giant was close behind. Faster and faster Jack climbed down—still clutching the golden hen in his arms. But as fast as he went, the giant seemed to go even faster.

Quickly Jack reached the ground and shouted to his mother.

JACK: [urgently] A hatchet. Get me a hatchet. Quickly. Quickly.

NARRATOR: His mother grabbed a hatchet and gave it to Jack. As fast as he could, Jack chopped at the beanstalk. Hacking and hacking—it finally fell with a mighty crash, killing the giant instantly.

MOTHER: Jack, you are safe!

JACK: Yes, mother. And I have brought you a fine gift—a hen that lays golden eggs.

NARRATOR: And so it was that Jack and his mother lived very happily and very well for the remainder of their lives.

The Princess and the Pea

STAGING: The narrator should be standing behind a lectern or a music stand to the side of the staging area. The other characters may be loosely assembled in the middle of the staging area. You may wish to place an old mattress or sleeping bag in the middle of the staging area.

				Narrator
				X
Prince	King	Queen	Princess	
X	X	X	X	

NARRATOR: Once upon a faraway time in a faraway kingdom there lived a prince. The prince was very lonely, and he wanted to marry a princess. But she had to be a *real* princess. Yes, she had to be a REAL princess.

PRINCE: Yes, I must have a real princess. Only a real princess will do.

NARRATOR: The prince looked and looked all over the kingdom. He met many beautiful maidens, but none of them was a real princess. So he sent all of them away.

One night there was a terrible storm. Rain was falling hard, lightning was slashing through the dark, and thunder was echoing across the hills. It was a most terrible storm. Suddenly, a knock was heard at the castle door.

QUEEN: Come in.

KING: Yes, come in.

NARRATOR: There before them stood a very wet girl. Her clothes were soaked and her hair was ragged.

PRINCESS: I would like to get out of this storm. May I spend the night here? I am a real princess, on my way home, when this storm came upon me. Would you have room for a real princess to stay the night?

QUEEN: A real princess, you say. I say that there is only one way to know if she is a real princess.

NARRATOR: The queen went off to make up a bed for the young lady.

PRINCE: I can only hope that she is a real princess. She is all wet and bedraggled now, but perhaps she is a real princess underneath all of that.

KING: I hope so, too, my son. I also hope that she is a real princess. You have been looking long and hard for a real princess. Who knows, maybe she is the princess you are seeking. If so, then your mother, the queen, will find out soon enough.

NARRATOR: The queen went into the guest room.

QUEEN: I shall place a tiny pea under the mattress. Then I shall have 20 more mattresses placed on top of the first mattress. There will be 21 mattresses on top of the tiny pea. If she is, indeed, a princess, then she will be able to feel the tiny pea under all 21 mattresses. Only a real princess will be able to feel a tiny pea under so many mattresses.

NARRATOR: And so the queen put 20 more mattresses on top of the first mattress: 1 . . . 2 . . . 3 . . . 4 . . . 5 . . . 6 . . . 7 . . . 8 . . . 9 . . . 10. More and more mattresses were piled on the bed. The bed grew higher and higher: 11 . . . 12 . . . 13 . . . 14 . . . 15 . . . 16 . . . 17 . . . 18 . . . 19 . . . 20. The bed was now 21 mattresses high.

QUEEN: Oh, princess, your bed is now ready. Come and sleep. You must be very tired.

PRINCESS: Thank you. Yes, I am very tired and looking forward to a long and restful sleep. Thank you very much.

NARRATOR: And so the princess crawled on top of all the mattresses and promptly fell asleep.

The next morning, everyone was sitting at the table eating their breakfast when the princess came in.

PRINCE: How did you sleep?

KING: Yes, how did you sleep last night?

QUEEN: How did you sleep? Yes, how did you sleep?

PRINCESS: I did not sleep very well. I felt a big lump in my bed all night long. It was because of that lump in my bed that I did not sleep very well.

NARRATOR: With that, both the king and the queen smiled. The prince was smiling, too.

KING: You must be a real princess!

PRINCE: Yes, you must be a real princess!

QUEEN: Yes, I know you are a real princess. That is because only a real princess could feel a pea under 21 mattresses!

NARRATOR: And so it came to pass that the prince married the real princess. And they lived forever in great happiness. And they kept the pea in a glass case in the castle museum.

Rapunzel

STAGING: The three narrators may each be seated on a high stool or chair at a music stand. The witch may walk around the staging area with a script in her hands.

Narrator 1	Narrator 2	Narrator 3
X	X	X
	Witch	
	X	

NARRATOR 1: In a small village a long, long time ago, there lived a woodcarver and his wife. For many years they had longed for a child and always hoped that some day their wish would come true.

NARRATOR 2: The young wife liked to sit in her window and look at the garden next door—a garden that just happened to belong to a witch. The garden was filled with wonderful flowers and beautiful vegetables. The young wife longed to have some of those plants—especially the rapunzel, or salad greens, that grew throughout the garden.

NARRATOR 3: She begged her husband to get her some rapunzel, fearing that she would die if she didn't have some. Eventually she grew weak and sickly, and her husband feared for her life.

NARRATOR 1: So one evening he climbed over the garden wall and into the witch's garden to get some rapunzel for his wife.

NARRATOR 2: No sooner had he began to collect the rapunzel than the witch appeared before him.

WITCH: What are you doing here in my garden, you thief?

NARRATOR 3: The young man begged for forgiveness from the witch. He told her how much his wife wanted the rapunzel and that she would die if she didn't get any.

WITCH: In that case, please help yourself. But for this favor I must demand a promise in return. You must give me your child when she is born. She will not be harmed, but have her I must.

NARRATOR 1: The young man was frightened, but he made the promise nonetheless. He gathered up the rapunzel and took it to his wife. As soon as she ate some of the delicious plant, she regained her health as well as her spirits.

NARRATOR 2: A year later a little girl was born to the couple. Within the hour the witch appeared and gathered the child in her arms and went away. She named the child Rapunzel, for the plant that had grown in her garden.

NARRATOR 3: Rapunzel grew up to be a very beautiful woman. Her hair, long and golden, grew so that it hung in a braid down to the floor.

NARRATOR 1: When Rapunzel turned 12, the witch took her to a high tower in the middle of the forest. There was neither a door nor a staircase in the tower. There was only a single window up under the roof. Whenever the witch wanted to visit Rapunzel, she would stand beneath the window and call:

WITCH: Rapunzel, Rapunzel,
Let down your golden hair.

NARRATOR 2: Rapunzel would tie her hair to a hook beside the window and throw her long braid down. The witch would then climb up the braid and into the window.

NARRATOR 3: Rapunzel spent three very lonely years in the tower. Only the animals of the forest were her friends.

NARRATOR 1: One bright summer day a prince came riding through the forest. While his horse was taking a drink, he heard a soft and beautiful sound coming through the trees. It was Rapunzel singing. The prince rode his horse over to the sound—the tall tower in the middle of the woods. He looked all around, but he could not find an entrance. So he decided to wait and see what would happen.

NARRATOR 2: In very short order he saw the witch coming through the woods. The witch went up to the tower and called out:

WITCH: Rapunzel, Rapunzel,
Let down your golden hair.

NARRATOR 3: Rapunzel did let down her golden hair as she was told. The witch quickly climbed up the hair. Hmmm, thought the prince, that is how I will get to the beautiful maiden.

NARRATOR 1: So the prince waited once more. Finally the witch climbed down Rapunzel's hair and went back to her cottage.

NARRATOR 2: The prince called out to Rapunzel to let down her golden hair, and in a short moment the golden hair came tumbling out of the tower. The prince climbed up the golden hair and stepped into the tower.

NARRATOR 3: Rapunzel was most surprised to see the prince standing there. The prince told her of the sweet songs he had heard in the woods and how he had discovered the source of that sweet music. He told her how much he loved the music and how much he loved her. He begged her to be his wife.

NARRATOR 1: Rapunzel was overcome with joy. She was also overcome with fear. She told the prince that the only way she could leave the tower would be if he brought a skein of silk each time he visited. Then Rapunzel could weave the silk into a ladder, with which they could both escape the tower.

NARRATOR 2: Rapunzel told the prince to come only in the evening, because the witch always visited during the day. The prince promised and soon rode off into the night.

NARRATOR 3: Each day the witch came, and each evening the prince came, bringing a skein of fine silk. When the witch was not there, Rapunzel wove the silk into a long and beautiful ladder.

NARRATOR 1: One day while the witch was visiting Rapunzel, she discovered the silk ladder in a corner of the tower.

WITCH: You wicked child! You wicked, wicked child! You have tried to deceive me. For that you will be punished.

NARRATOR 2: With that the witch took a pair of scissors and cut off Rapunzel's long hair. Then she banished Rapunzel to a wilderness far, far away.

NARRATOR 3: That evening the witch tied Rapunzel's golden locks to a hook beside the window and let them down the side of the tower. Soon the prince came by and called for Rapunzel.

NARRATOR 1: The wicked witch dropped the long braids out the window. When the prince climbed up them, he found himself face to face with the witch.

WITCH: So, you have come to see the beautiful princess. I'm afraid she is gone forever. She has flown away, and you will never see her again. Ha, ha, ha!

NARRATOR 2: The prince was so upset that he leaped out of the high tower. He fell into a thorn bush, scratching his eyes so much that he was blinded.

NARRATOR 3: The prince wandered over the countryside for two years, until one special day he came to the place where Rapunzel was resting. Rapunzel quickly recognized the prince, even though he was in rags and blind. She cried tears of joy for him. When her tears fell on his blinded eyes, his sight was restored. They then journeyed to the prince's castle, where they were married and where they both lived happily ever after.

Rumpelstiltskin

STAGING: The characters may all be placed behind music stands. The daughter may be seated in a chair, holding her script in her hands. If possible, place a wheel of some kind (an old bicycle wheel, for example) in front of the daughter to serve as a makeshift spinning wheel.

Narrator X				
	Miller X	King X	Daughter/Queen X	
				Dwarf X

NARRATOR: Once upon a time, in a far off land, there lived a miller and his daughter. The daughter was very beautiful, and the miller would always boast about her great beauty. One day while the miller was doing some business at the castle, he happened to speak with the young king.

MILLER: I have a very beautiful daughter, who would make someone a fine wife. Not only is she very beautiful, but she is equally clever as well.

KING: Please tell me more.

MILLER: My beautiful daughter is so clever that she can spin straw into gold.

KING: That is very hard to believe, but if it is true, then I shall be more than happy to make her my bride.

MILLER: Then I will make it so.

KING: Very well. Send your daughter to the castle tomorrow morning, and we shall see just how clever she is.

NARRATOR: And so the next morning the beautiful daughter arrived at the castle. She was led to a room full of straw.

KING: There is your work before you. In one day's time you must spin all this straw into gold. If you do not, then you shall die.

NARRATOR: The miller's daughter sat down at her spinning wheel and began to cry.

DAUGHTER: [crying] What shall I do? I am an excellent spinner, but not even I can spin straw into gold.

NARRATOR: Suddenly the door sprang open, and an old dwarf stepped into the room.

DWARF: Hello, young maiden. Why are you crying so?

DAUGHTER: I have been told that I must spin this straw into gold. If not, then I shall die. I don't know how to do it!

DWARF: What would it be worth to you if I should do it?

DAUGHTER: I will give you my pearl necklace.

DWARF: Very well.

NARRATOR: The dwarf put the necklace in his pocket. He then sat down at the spinning wheel and began to spin the straw into gold. The next morning when the king came to check on the daughter, he found the room filled with gold. Being somewhat greedy, he decided to give her a larger task. He led the miller's daughter to another room—this one filled even higher and even deeper with straw. He ordered her to spin it all into gold or she would die when the morning came. After he left she fell to her knees, weeping.

DAUGHTER: [crying] Oh, what will I do? What will I do?

NARRATOR: Just as before, the dwarf appeared in the room offering to help the young girl. And just as before, the dwarf wanted something in return.

DAUGHTER: I will give you my silver ring.

DWARF: Very well. That will do.

NARRATOR: Once again, the dwarf sat down at the spinning wheel and spun all the straw into gold. At dawn, when the king returned, he was even more amazed at what he saw. But he wanted even more. So for a third time he placed the miller's daughter in a very large room, overflowing with straw.

KING: This time, if you should spin all this straw into gold before the morning, I shall make you my queen. However, if you fail, you will die.

NARRATOR: Once again the miller's daughter broke down in tears. And once again, the dwarf appeared in the doorway.

DAUGHTER: I have nothing more to give you.

DWARF: Then promise me your first-born child when you become queen.

NARRATOR: Not knowing what to do, she reluctantly promised the dwarf her first-born child. In the morning when the king returned, he saw a room filled to the rafters with gold. He was so overcome with happiness that he proposed to the miller's daughter, and they were married at once.

NARRATOR: A year went by, and a young boy was born to the queen. By then she had forgotten about her promise to the dwarf. And then one day the door swung open, and the dwarf appeared before her.

DWARF: Remember the promise you gave me? I have come for your child.

NARRATOR: The queen begged and begged him not to take her child. She offered him riches. He said, "No." She offered him land. He said, "No." She offered him everything she could think of—each time he said, "No."

DWARF: All that means nothing to me. You promised me your child, and I have come to take him.

QUEEN: There must be something else. Please, please, there must be another way!

DWARF: Very well. I will give you three days. Within those three days you must discover my name. If you do, you may keep your child. If you do not, then the child shall be mine.

NARRATOR: The queen sent messengers all across the kingdom to try to discover the name of the dwarf. The next day the dwarf appeared in her doorway.

QUEEN: Is your name Michael? Is it Obed? Is it Humpty-back?

DWARF: No, no, no.

NARRATOR: The queen sent more messengers and more servants across the land to discover the name of the dwarf. They traveled far and they traveled wide and brought back all manner of names. On the evening of the second day the dwarf appeared once again.

QUEEN: Is your name Spiderlegs? Is your name Gilbert? Is your name Ronald?

DWARF: No, no, no. My name is none of those.

NARRATOR: Now, the queen was in a terrible state. The third day everyone in the kingdom was searching for the name of the dwarf. Just as evening fell, one of her servants ran up to her and told her about a small hut he had found deep in the woods. He had seen a bright fire in front of the hut, and around the fire was a little man dancing with a black cat. As the two of them danced, the little man sang a song.

DWARF: I can dance and I can sing.
Tomorrow brings my little king!
The servants look both high and low.
They'll never find my name, I know.
For I control this little game,
And Rumpelstiltskin is my name.

NARRATOR: Later that night the door burst open and the dwarf entered the queen's chamber.

DWARF: Well, my queen, what is my name?

QUEEN: Is your name John?

DWARF: NO!

QUEEN: Is your name Rupert?

DWARF: NO! NO!

QUEEN: Hmmm, is there a chance that your name is . . . is . . . Rumpelstiltskin?

NARRATOR: The dwarf was furious. He was mad. He was angry. He stamped his foot so hard that he went right through the floor—splitting himself in half. And in a twinkle he was never seen again. And of course the queen and her son were to live lives of great joy and happiness.

Snow White and the Seven Dwarfs

STAGING: The three narrators should be placed in the rear of the staging area. They should each be standing behind a music stand or lectern. The other characters may walk around the staging area with scripts in their hands.

Narrator 1		Narrator 2		Narrator 3
X		X		X
	Stepmother	Snow White	Chief Dwarf	
	X	X	X	

NARRATOR 1: Once upon a time there lived in a great castle a beautiful maiden. She was quite pretty, with blue eyes and long, flowing hair. Her skin was delicate and pale, so she was called Snow White.

NARRATOR 2: However, she also had a very evil stepmother—a stepmother who was very jealous of Snow White's beauty.

NARRATOR 3: Every day the evil stepmother would stand in front of her mirror and ask the mirror a single question.

STEPMOTHER: Mirror, mirror, on the wall,
Who is the fairest one of all?

NARRATOR 1: The mirror always answered that the stepmother was, indeed, the most beautiful one in the whole kingdom.

NARRATOR 2: But, alas, one day the mirror told the evil stepmother that Snow White was now the most beautiful creature in the whole kingdom.

NARRATOR 3: As you might imagine, this made the evil stepmother very, very angry.

STEPMOTHER: [very angrily] Who does she think she is? She cannot be the most beautiful creature in the kingdom. *I* am the most beautiful. Snow White must die.

NARRATOR 1: And so the evil stepmother called one of her servants and told him to take Snow White deep into the forest and slay her.

NARRATOR 2: The servant put Snow White on a horse and led her into the deepest and darkest part of the forest.

NARRATOR 3: But he was overcome with guilt and could not kill this innocent maiden. So he left her in the forest, beside a tall tree, and hastened away. Snow White was all alone.

SNOW WHITE: [crying] It is so dark here. It is so lonely here. There are many strange sounds. I am very afraid.

NARRATOR 1: Finally Snow White fell asleep. At dawn the sounds of birds woke her. She looked around and saw many animals scurrying about.

NARRATOR 2: She soon found a path in the woods and began to walk along it. Before long she came to a meadow wherein stood a small cottage with a tiny door, tiny windows, and a tiny chimney.

NARRATOR 3: Snow White walked up to the very small cottage and knocked on the door. Nobody answered, so she pushed the door open and walked in.

SNOW WHITE: What a tiny, tiny place. And, look, there's a tiny table with seven tiny plates on it. Indeed, this table is set for seven people.

NARRATOR 1: Snow White went upstairs, where she found seven tiny beds. When she came back downstairs she had an idea.

SNOW WHITE: I know, I'll fix them all a fine dinner to eat. When they all come home, they'll have a fine meal before them.

NARRATOR 2: Soon there was a sound coming from the forest. It was the sound of people singing. Suddenly seven little men burst through the door of the cottage.

NARRATOR 3: To their surprise they found hot, steaming owls of soup on the table. And the whole house had been cleaned from top to bottom.

CHIEF DWARF: [to Snow White] Who are you, and what are you doing here?

SNOW WHITE: My name is Snow White. I live in a faraway kingdom, and my evil stepmother wanted me killed because she is jealous of my beauty. I was taken into the forest by one of her servants, but he could not kill me. So he left me there and I eventually found my way here.

CHIEF DWARF: Very well. You may stay here with us. You can tend to the house while we work in the mines. You do not have to worry about your evil stepmother. We will take care of you and watch over you. You will be safe here.

NARRATOR 1: All the dwarfs jumped up and down and cheered for joy. They were all very happy to have Snow White stay with them.

NARRATOR 2: The next morning the seven dwarfs set off to work in the mines. Before they left they told Snow White to never open the door to any strangers.

NARRATOR 3: Meanwhile, the servant had returned to the castle. He told the evil stepmother that he had killed Snow White just as he had been commanded.

NARRATOR 1: Being very pleased, the evil stepmother turned to her magic mirror and asked it a question.

STEPMOTHER: Mirror, mirror, on the wall,
Who is the fairest one of all?

NARRATOR 2: Thinking that the mirror would answer that she, the evil stepmother, was the most beautiful one in the kingdom, she was quite surprised when the mirror told her that Snow White was still the prettiest.

STEPMOTHER: [very angrily] Oh, darn! Oh, drat! I must now go and teach that little girl a lesson she will never forget. She must die! SHE MUST DIE!!

NARRATOR 3: The stepmother disguised herself as an old peasant woman and filled a basket with apples, including one that had been poisoned.

NARRATOR 1: She climbed on her horse and rode off into the woods. Crossing a stream, she came upon the tiny cottage and knocked on the door.

SNOW WHITE: Who's there?

STEPMOTHER: It is just me. I'm an old peasant woman selling apples to make a living. Would you like an apple?

SNOW WHITE: I do not need any apples, thank you.

STEPMOTHER: But these are very fine apples. And they are quite delicious!

SNOW WHITE: I must not open the door to anyone. So thank you very much.

STEPMOTHER: Very well, I understand. But in case you change your mind, I shall leave one of my finest apples here by the door.

NARRATOR 2: With that the evil stepmother hurried back to the castle. Filled with curiosity, Snow White opened the door a crack and saw the apple on the porch.

NARRATOR 3: She grabbed the apple, slammed the door closed, and, being quite hungry, took a large bite from the apple.

NARRATOR 1: Instantly Snow White fell into a deep, deep sleep. The effects of the poison apple made her a lifeless form.

NARRATOR 2: That afternoon the dwarfs returned home from a day of working in the mines. There they found Snow White, lying lifeless and still on the floor of the tiny cottage.

NARRATOR 3: The dwarfs cried and cried. They carried her into the forest and gently placed her on a bed of rose petals.

NARRATOR 1: Each day they brought a rose and gently placed it beside the sleeping body of Snow White.

NARRATOR 2: Then one day, when they came to place their rose, they saw a young prince standing over Snow White.

CHIEF DWARF: That is Snow White. She has bitten into a poisoned apple and now is fast asleep. She sleeps here forever.

NARRATOR 3: The young prince took great pity on the beautiful maiden. He bent down and placed a gentle kiss on her lips.

NARRATOR 1: With that, the spell from the poisoned apple was broken. Snow White awoke from her sleep to discover the handsome prince standing before her.

NARRATOR 2: The young prince immediately asked Snow White to marry him and to live with him in a great castle.

NARRATOR 3: Snow White agreed. She said good-bye to the seven dwarfs and went to live with the handsome prince—happily ever after!

The Little Red Hen

STAGING: The characters should all be placed behind music stands or lecterns. The narrator may be placed off to the side and away from the other characters.

	Dog X	Goose X	Cat X	
Little Red Hen X				
				Narrator X

NARRATOR: Once upon a time there was a little red hen. She lived on a farm with a dog, a goose, and a cat.

One day the little red hen found some grains of wheat on the ground.

LITTLE RED HEN: Who will help me plant this wheat?

DOG: Not I!

GOOSE: Not I!

CAT: Not I!

LITTLE RED HEN: OK, then I will plant it myself.

NARRATOR: And she did!

The Little Red Hen watered and weeded and watched. She watched as the wheat began to grow. The wheat grew and grew until it was very tall. Finally the wheat was ready to be cut.

LITTLE RED HEN: Who will help me cut the wheat?

DOG: Not I!

GOOSE: Not I!

CAT: Not I!

LITTLE RED HEN: OK, then I will cut it myself.

NARRATOR: And she did!

The Little Red Hen cut and cut and cut the wheat. She cut down all the wheat and gathered it into a large pile. There was a lot of wheat in the pile. The wheat was ready to be beat.

LITTLE RED HEN: Who will help me beat the wheat?

DOG: Not I!

GOOSE: Not I!

CAT: Not I!

LITTLE RED HEN: OK, then I will beat it myself.

NARRATOR: And she did!

The Little Red Hen beat and beat and beat. She beat all the wheat until all the kernels had fallen out of the wheat. There was a large pile of kernels. The wheat was ready to be shipped to the mill.

LITTLE RED HEN: Who will help me take the wheat to the mill?

DOG: Not I!

GOOSE: Not I!

CAT: Not I!

LITTLE RED HEN: OK, then I will take it myself.

NARRATOR: And she did!

The Little Red Hen took the wheat to the mill. There it was ground into flour. All the flour was put in a large sack. The Little Red Hen brought the large sack of flour back home.

LITTLE RED HEN: Who will help me bake the bread?

DOG: Not I!

GOOSE: Not I!

CAT: Not I!

LITTLE RED HEN: OK, then I will bake it myself.

NARRATOR: And she did!

The Little Red Hen baked the bread in the oven until it was a toasty brown. The good smell filled the house. When the bread came out of the oven it smelled very good . . . very, very good!

The dog, the goose, and the cat smelled the bread. They ran to the house to get some. The Little Red Hen put the bread on the table.

LITTLE RED HEN: Who will help me eat this good bread?

DOG: I will!

GOOSE: I will!

CAT: I will!

LITTLE RED HEN: Oh, no, you won't!

NARRATOR: And she ate up all the bread herself.

The Gingerbread Man

STAGING: The two narrators may stand at lecterns or podiums on both sides of the staging area. The other characters may stand in a random pattern across the staging area. The Gingerbread Man may wish to move back and forth across the staging area each time he says, "Run, run, as fast as you can . . . ."

```
        Cow        Horse      Thresher        Mower
         X           X           X              X

   Little Old Woman                      Little Old Man
         X                                     X
                        Gingerbread Man
                              X        Fox
                                        X
   Narrator 1                                  Narrator 2
       X                                           X
```

NARRATOR 1: Once upon a time there was a Little Old Woman . . . .

LITTLE OLD WOMAN: That's me!

NARRATOR 2: . . . and a Little Old Man.

LITTLE OLD MAN: That's me!

NARRATOR 1: Well, they both lived in a little old house in the middle of the little old woods. They were very lonely, so one day the Little Old Woman decided to make a Gingerbread Boy.

NARRATOR 2: So she rolled out some gingerbread, sprinkled it with cinnamon, used some raisins for his eyes, and made his mouth out of rose-colored sugar. She put him on a pan and put him in the oven.

NARRATOR 1: After a time she opened the oven door and took out the pan.

LITTLE OLD WOMAN: That's what I did—I took out the pan!

LITTLE OLD MAN: Yes, she took out the pan.

NARRATOR 2: Just as she took out the pan, the little Gingerbread Boy jumped onto the floor and ran out the door.

NARRATOR 1: The Little Old Woman and the Little Old Man ran after the Gingerbread Boy. But the Gingerbread Boy was much too fast, and he ran down the road, laughing and shouting.

GINGERBREAD BOY: Run, run as fast as you can! You can't catch me, I'm the Gingerbread Man!

NARRATOR 2: And they couldn't catch him.

NARRATOR 1: The Gingerbread Boy ran down the road. Finally he came to a large field with a cow in it.

COW: Stop, little Gingerbread Boy. I want to eat you!

GINGERBREAD BOY: I have run away from a Little Old Man and a Little Old Woman, and I can run away from you, I can!

NARRATOR 2: The cow chased him down the road. But the Gingerbread Boy just looked over his shoulder and cried,

GINGERBREAD BOY: Run, run as fast as you can! You can't catch me, I'm the Gingerbread Man!

NARRATOR 1: And the cow couldn't catch him.

NARRATOR 2:	The little Gingerbread Boy ran on and on, until he came to a horse in a pasture.
HORSE:	Please stop, Little Gingerbread Boy. You look good enough to eat.
GINGERBREAD BOY:	Oh, no. I have run away from a Little Old Man and a Little Old Woman and a cow, and I can run away from you, I can!
NARRATOR 1:	The horse chased him down the road. But the Gingerbread Boy just looked over his shoulder and cried,
GINGERBREAD BOY:	Run, run as fast as you can! You can't catch me, I'm the Gingerbread Man!
NARRATOR 2:	And the horse couldn't catch him.
NARRATOR 1:	By and by the little Gingerbread Boy came to a barn where a thresher was working.
THRESHER:	Please stop, little Gingerbread Boy. You look good enough to eat.
GINGERBREAD BOY:	Oh, no. I have run away from a Little Old Man and a Little Old Woman and a cow and a horse, and I can run away from you, I can!
NARRATOR 2:	The thresher chased him down the road. But the Gingerbread Boy just looked over his shoulder and cried,
GINGERBREAD BOY:	Run, run as fast as you can! You can't catch me, I'm the Gingerbread Man!
NARRATOR 1:	And the thresher couldn't catch him.
NARRATOR 2:	By and by the little Gingerbread Boy came to a field where a mower was working.
MOWER:	Please stop, little Gingerbread Boy. You look good enough to eat.

GINGERBREAD BOY: Oh, no. I have run away from a Little Old Man and a Little Old Woman and a cow and a horse and a thresher, and I can run away from you, I can!

NARRATOR 1: The mower chased him down the road. But the Gingerbread Boy just looked over his shoulder and cried,

GINGERBREAD BOY: Run, run as fast as you can! You can't catch me, I'm the Gingerbread Man!

NARRATOR 2: And the mower couldn't catch him.

NARRATOR 1: By and by the little Gingerbread Boy came to a fox who was walking down the road.

GINGERBREAD BOY: I have run away from a Little Old Man and a Little Old Woman and a cow and a horse and a thresher and a mower, and I can run away from you, I can! Run, run as fast as you can! You can't catch me, I'm the Gingerbread Man!

FOX: Why, I am not interested in catching you. I would not think of such a thing!

NARRATOR 2: Just then the little Gingerbread Boy came to a river. He could not swim across.

NARRATOR 1: But he wanted to keep running away from all the animals and all the people who were chasing him.

FOX: Hey, little Gingerbread Boy, why don't you jump on my tail, and I will take you across the river?

NARRATOR 2: So the little Gingerbread Boy jumped on the fox's tail, and the fox swam into the river. When he was a short distance from shore, he turned his head and said,

FOX: You are too heavy on my tail, little Gingerbread Boy. I'm afraid you will get wet. Why don't you jump on my back?

NARRATOR 1: So the little Gingerbread Boy jumped on the fox's back.

NARRATOR 2: The fox swam a little further out into the river and said to the little Gingerbread Boy,

FOX: I'm afraid the water will cover you there. Why don't you jump on my shoulder?

NARRATOR 1: So the little Gingerbread Boy jumped on the fox's shoulder.

NARRATOR 2: In the middle of the river, the fox said to the little Gingerbread Boy,

FOX: Oh, no, my shoulder is sinking. Why don't you jump on my nose?

NARRATOR 1: So the little Gingerbread Boy jumped on the fox's . . .

NARRATOR 2: SNAP! SNAP! SNAP!

NARRATOR 1: And just like that, the little Gingerbread Boy was gone!

NARRATOR 2: And he never ever said anything again.

FOX: Run, run, little Gingerbread Man. I'm a hungry fox, and I can eat you, I can!

Goldilocks and the Three Bears

STAGING: The narrators and the three bears may all be seated on tall stools or chairs. Each should be behind a music stand or lectern. Goldilocks should hold a script in her hands and walk around the staging area.

	Papa Bear X	Mama Bear X	Baby Bear X
Goldilocks X			
Narrator 1 X			Narrator 2 X

NARRATOR 1: Once upon a time, in a faraway place, there lived a family of bears. There was Papa Bear . . .

PAPA BEAR: That's me!

NARRATOR: . . . Momma Bear . . .

MAMA BEAR: That's me!

NARRATOR: . . . and Baby Bear.

BABY BEAR: That's me!

NARRATOR 2: The three bears lived in a very large cottage in the middle of the woods. They were a happy bear family—they played together, they laughed together, and they went for lots of walks in the woods together. They didn't bother anyone, and nobody bothered them.

NARRATOR 1: Well, one day a little girl named Goldilocks . . .

GOLDILOCKS: That's me!

NARRATOR 1: . . . decided to go for a walk in the woods. She had never walked in the woods before, and she was curious about what she might find there.

NARRATOR 2: At the same time, Mama Bear was working in her kitchen.

MAMA BEAR: I'm making a fine porridge for us to eat. But, in taking it out of the oven I notice that it is very hot. It is far too hot to eat.

PAPA BEAR: Well then, we should go for a walk in the woods while the porridge is cooling.

BABY BEAR: That sounds like fun. Let's go!

NARRATOR 2: And so the three bears left the porridge on the table to cool and went for a walk in the woods.

NARRATOR 1: Meanwhile, Goldilocks was coming down the path. As she turned the corner she saw the three bears' cottage. She walked up to the cottage and peered in the windows. As she looked inside she saw the three bowls of porridge on the table. She was very hungry and decided that she wanted some porridge.

GOLDILOCKS: Yes, I am very hungry and should like to have some porridge to eat.

NARRATOR 2: So Goldilocks opened the door of the cottage and walked inside. She dipped her fingers into Papa Bear's bowl of porridge.

GOLDILOCKS: Ohhhh, this is way too hot! It is much too hot for me to eat.

NARRATOR 1: Then she dipped her fingers into Mama Bear's porridge.

GOLDILOCKS: Ohhh, this is way too cool! It is much too cool for me to eat.

NARRATOR 2: Then she dipped her fingers into Baby Bear's porridge.

GOLDILOCKS: Ahhhh, this is just right!

NARRATOR 1: And with that, she ate up all the porridge in Baby Bear's bowl.

NARRATOR 2: Walking around inside the cottage, Goldilocks came upon the three chairs belonging to the three bears.

NARRATOR 1: First she sat down in Papa Bear's chair.

GOLDILOCKS: Ohhhh, this is much too big!

NARRATOR 2: Then she sat down in Mama Bear's chair.

GOLDILOCKS: Ohhhh, this is much too narrow!

NARRATOR 1: Then she sat down in Baby Bear's chair.

GOLDILOCKS: Ahhhh, this is just right!

NARRATOR 2: After a while, Goldilocks decided to go upstairs and see what she could find. There she found the three bears' beds.

NARRATOR 1: First she lay down in Papa Bear's bed.

GOLDILOCKS: Ohhhh, this is much too soft!

NARRATOR 2: Then she lay down in Mama Bear's bed!

GOLDILOCKS: Ohhhh, this is much too hard.

NARRATOR 1: Then she lay down in Baby Bear's bed.

GOLDILOCKS: Ahhhh, this is just right!

NARRATOR 2: And she fell fast asleep.

NARRATOR 1: Before long, the three bears came back from their walk in the woods. As soon as they walked in the door, they could see that something was wrong.

PAPA BEAR: Who's been eating my porridge?

MAMA BEAR: Who's been eating my porridge?

BABY BEAR: Who's been eating my porridge? And it's all gone!

NARRATOR 2: The three bears went into the living room. As soon as they walked in, they could see that something was wrong.

PAPA BEAR: Who's been sitting in my chair?

MAMA BEAR: Who's been sitting in my chair?

BABY BEAR: Who's been sitting in my chair? And it's all broken!

NARRATOR 1: Then the three bears went upstairs. As soon as they walked into the bedroom, they could see that something was wrong.

PAPA BEAR: Who's been sleeping in my bed?

MAMA BEAR: Who's been sleeping in my bed?

BABY BEAR: Who's been sleeping in my bed? And she's right there!

NARRATOR 2: With that, Goldilocks woke up. When she saw the three bears standing over her, she was so frightened that she ran as fast as she could away from the house.

PAPA BEAR: Who's running away from our house?

MAMA BEAR: Who's running away from our house?

BABY BEAR: Who's running away from our house? And there she goes!

Chicken Little

STAGING: The characters should all be holding their scripts in their hands. Encourage them to move around the staging area (everyone gets behind Chicken Little and follows him or her throughout the production). Because there are several characters in this rendition, you may wish to do one or two practice sessions before a more formal presentation.

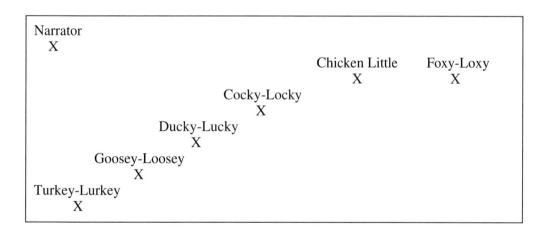

NARRATOR: One fine day, Chicken Little decided to go for a walk. As she was walking through the woods, an acorn fell right on top of her head. She was so scared that she shook and shook and shook. In fact, she shook so much that half of her feathers fell out.

CHICKEN LITTLE: [loudly and excitedly] The sky is falling! The sky is falling! I have to go tell the king that the sky is falling. The sky is falling! THE SKY IS FALLING!

NARRATOR: And so she ran as fast as she could to go tell the king that the sky was falling. Along the way she met Cocky-Locky.

COCKY-LOCKY: Where are you going, Chicken Little?

CHICKEN LITTLE: [excitedly] I'm going to tell the king that the sky is falling, the sky is falling!

COCKY-LOCKY: How do you know the sky is falling, Chicken Little?

CHICKEN LITTLE: I felt it on my head! I felt it on my head! I felt the sky falling on my head!

COCKY-LOCKY: This is terrible! This is just terrible! We have to go tell the king that the sky is falling, the sky is falling!

NARRATOR: And so Chicken Little and Cocky-Locky ran as fast as they could through the woods. Pretty soon they met Ducky-Lucky.

DUCKY-LUCKY: Where are you going, Chicken Little? Where are you going, Cocky-Locky?

CHICKEN LITTLE: [excitedly] The sky is falling! THE SKY IS FALLING! We're going to tell the king that the sky is falling!

COCKY-LOCKY: [excitedly] The sky is falling! THE SKY IS FALLING! We're going to tell the king that the sky is falling!

DUCKY-LUCKY: How do you know the sky is falling, Chicken Little? How do you know the sky is falling, Cocky-Locky?

CHICKEN LITTLE: I felt it on my head! I felt it on my head! I felt the sky falling on my head!

COCKY-LOCKY: Chicken Little felt it on her head! She felt it on her head! She felt the sky falling on her head!

DUCKY-LUCKY: This is terrible! This is just terrible! We have to go tell the king that the sky is falling, the sky is falling!

NARRATOR: And so Chicken Little and Cocky-Locky and Ducky-Lucky ran as fast as they could through the woods. Pretty soon they met Goosey-Loosey.

GOOSEY-LOOSEY: Where are you going, Chicken Little? Where are you going, Cocky-Locky? Where are you going, Ducky-Lucky?

CHICKEN LITTLE: [excitedly] The sky is falling! THE SKY IS FALLING! We're going to tell the king that the sky is falling!

COCKY-LOCKY: [excitedly] The sky is falling! THE SKY IS FALLING! We're going to tell the king that the sky is falling!

DUCKY-LUCKY: [excitedly] The sky is falling! THE SKY IS FALLING! We're going to tell the king that the sky is falling!

GOOSEY-LOOSEY: How do you know the sky is falling, Chicken Little? How do you know the sky is falling, Cocky-Locky? How do you know the sky is falling, Ducky-Lucky?

CHICKEN LITTLE: I felt it on my head! I felt it on my head! I felt the sky falling on my head!

COCKY-LOCKY: Chicken Little felt it on her head! She felt it on her head! She felt the sky falling on her head!

DUCKY-LUCKY: Chicken Little felt it on her head! She felt it on her head! She felt the sky falling on her head!

GOOSEY-LOOSEY: This is terrible! This is just terrible! We have to go tell the king that the sky is falling, the sky is falling!

NARRATOR: And so Chicken Little and Cocky-Locky and Ducky-Lucky and Goosey-Loosey ran as fast as they could through the woods. Pretty soon they met Turkey-Lurkey.

TURKEY-LURKEY:	Where are you going, Chicken Little? Where are you going, Cocky-Locky? Where are you going, Ducky-Lucky? Where are you going, Goosey-Loosey?
CHICKEN LITTLE:	[excitedly] The sky is falling! THE SKY IS FALLING! We're going to tell the king that the sky is falling!
COCKY-LOCKY:	[excitedly] The sky is falling! THE SKY IS FALLING! We're going to tell the king that the sky is falling!
DUCKY-LUCKY:	[excitedly] The sky is falling! THE SKY IS FALLING! We're going to tell the king that the sky is falling!
GOOSEY-LOOSEY:	[excitedly] The sky is falling! THE SKY IS FALLING! We're going to tell the king that the sky is falling!
TURKEY-LURKEY:	How do you know the sky is falling, Chicken Little? How do you know the sky is falling, Cocky-Locky? How do you know the sky is falling, Ducky-Lucky? How do you know the sky is falling, Goosey-Loosey?
CHICKEN LITTLE:	I felt it on my head! I felt it on my head! I felt the sky falling on my head!
COCKY-LOCKY:	Chicken Little felt it on her head! She felt it on her head! She felt the sky falling on her head!
DUCKY-LUCKY:	Chicken Little felt it on her head! She felt it on her head! She felt the sky falling on her head!
GOOSEY-LOOSEY:	Chicken Little felt it on her head! She felt it on her head! She felt the sky falling on her head!
TURKEY-LURKEY:	This is terrible! This is just terrible! We have to go tell the king that the sky is falling, the sky is falling!

NARRATOR:	And so Chicken Little and Cocky-Locky and Ducky-Lucky and Goosey-Loosey and Turkey-Lurkey ran as fast as they could through the woods. Pretty soon they met Foxy-Loxy.
FOXY-LOXY:	Where are you going, Chicken Little? Where are you going, Cocky-Locky? Where are you going, Ducky-Lucky? Where are you going, Goosey-Loosey? Where are you going, Turkey-Lurkey?
CHICKEN LITTLE:	[excitedly] The sky is falling! THE SKY IS FALLING! We're going to tell the king that the sky is falling!
COCKY-LOCKY:	[excitedly] The sky is falling! THE SKY IS FALLING! We're going to tell the king that the sky is falling!
DUCKY-LUCKY:	[excitedly] The sky is falling! THE SKY IS FALLING! We're going to tell the king that the sky is falling!
GOOSEY-LOOSEY:	[excitedly] The sky is falling! THE SKY IS FALLING! We're going to tell the king that the sky is falling!
TURKEY-LURKEY:	[excitedly] The sky is falling! THE SKY IS FALLING! We're going to tell the king that the sky is falling!
FOXY-LOXY:	How do you know the sky is falling, Chicken Little? How do you know the sky is falling, Cocky-Locky? How do you know the sky is falling, Ducky-Lucky? How do you know the sky is falling, Goosey-Loosey? How do you know the sky is falling, Turkey-Lurkey?
CHICKEN LITTLE:	I felt it on my head! I felt it on my head! I felt the sky falling on my head!
COCKY-LOCKY:	Chicken Little felt it on her head! She felt it on her head! She felt the sky falling on her head!

75

DUCKY-LUCKY: Chicken Little felt it on her head! She felt it on her head! She felt the sky falling on her head!

GOOSEY-LOOSEY: Chicken Little felt it on her head! She felt it on her head! She felt the sky falling on her head!

TURKEY-LURKEY: Chicken Little felt it on her head! She felt it on her head! She felt the sky falling on her head!

FOXY-LOXY: Well, this is just terrible. But you are going the wrong way to see the king. Follow me, and I will show you the right way to get to the king so you can tell him that the sky is falling.

CHICKEN LITTLE: Very well!

COCKY-LOCKY: Very well!

DUCKY-LUCKY: Very well!

GOOSEY-LOOSEY: Very well!

TURKEY-LURKEY: Very well!

NARRATOR: So Foxy Loxy led Chicken Little, Cocky-Locky, Ducky-Lucky, Goosey-Loosey, and Turkey-Lurkey across a wide field and through the deep, dark woods. He led them all straight into his den, where he had a very fine dinner . . . a very fine dinner, indeed! And they never got to tell the king that the sky was falling, the sky was falling!

Little Red Riding Hood

STAGING: The characters may stand at podiums or music stands. The wolf and Red Riding Hood may wish to "walk" over to Granny and the hunter for the later parts of the production. The narrator should be standing off to the side for the entire production.

	Red Riding Hood X		Wolf X	
Narrator X		Granny X		Hunter X

NARRATOR: Once upon a time there lived a little girl by the name of Little Red Riding Hood. One day she decided that she wanted to visit her dear grandmother, who lived on the other side of the woods.

LITTLE RED RIDING HOOD: I haven't seen my grandmother for quite some time. I think I shall take her a basket of treats.

NARRATOR: The woods were very dangerous, and there were lots of creatures that lived in the woods—like wolves. But Red Riding Hood decided it was a good idea to see her grandmother. She just hoped that she wouldn't see any wolves in the woods.

So she set out with her basket. She walked through the woods, and before long a very large wolf jumped out from behind a tree.

WOLF: Good day, Little Red Riding Hood. Where are you off to?

LITTLE RED RIDING HOOD: I am off to see my grandmother, who lives on the other side of the woods. I am bringing her some treats, and we shall have a picnic.

WOLF: That is very well. I hope you are safe and that you take your time as you walk in the woods.

NARRATOR: Little Red Riding Hood continued down the trail. Meanwhile the wolf decided that he could have some fun and, perhaps, a meal for himself as well. He ran through the woods and arrived at Granny's house long before Little Red Riding Hood. He knocked on the door.

GRANNY: Who's there?

WOLF: It's just me. I am lost and hope that you might be able to help me with some directions.

GRANNY: Very well. I shall be glad to assist you with some directions.

NARRATOR: With that, Granny opened the door. Before she knew it, the wolf had gobbled her up and had himself a very good meal. Then he quickly slipped into Granny's pajamas and jumped into her bed. Before long Little Red Riding Hood arrived at the house and knocked on the door.

WOLF: Who's there?

LITTLE RED RIDING HOOD: It's me, Granny. I have a basket filled with all kinds of goodies. I thought you might like to have a picnic.

WOLF: Well, why didn't you say so? Come right in.

NARRATOR: And so Little Red Riding Hood entered the house. And there in the bed was the wolf, dressed up in Granny's pajamas.

LITTLE RED RIDING HOOD: My, Granny, what big ears you have.

WOLF: The better to listen to you, my dear.

LITTLE RED RIDING HOOD: My, Granny, what big eyes you have.

WOLF: The better to see you, my dear.

LITTLE RED RIDING HOOD: My, Granny, what big teeth you have.

GRANNY: The better to eat you, my dear.

NARRATOR: With that, the wolf jumped out of the bed and gobbled up Little Red Riding Hood just like he had her grandmother. But before he finished, Little Red Riding Hood let out a loud scream. A nearby hunter heard the scream and ran to the house.

HUNTER: Hey, what was that scream?

NARRATOR: Just as the hunter entered the house, he saw the wolf all dressed up in Granny's pajamas. Right away he knew what had happened, and he took his gun and killed the wolf. With a very sharp knife he cut open the wolf's belly, and out stepped Little red Riding Hood and Granny.

LITTLE RED RIDING HOOD: You saved us. YOU SAVED US!

GRANNY: Yes, you saved us. Thank you very much.

HUNTER: I'm glad I could save you from the wolf.

NARRATOR: From that day on Little Red Riding Hood always remembered that she should never talk to strangers—particularly large, furry strangers who lived in the woods.

The Three Little Pigs

STAGING: All the characters should be placed behind music stands or lecterns. The wolf may wish to move around the stage—from character to character—as the play evolves.

```
Narrator
  X
              Pig 1            Pig 2            Pig 3
               X                X                X
                                                      Wolf
                                                       X
```

NARRATOR: Once upon a time there were three little pigs. They liked to play in the mud and dance in the street and laugh all day long. There came a day when the three pigs decided that they wanted to see the world. So they left their mother and father and set off down the road. They had traveled some distance when they decided that they each needed to build a home to live in.

PIG 1: I shall build my house of straw. It will be a very easy house to build. It will not take much time, and I should be able to complete it in less than a day.

PIG 2: That will never do. Your house will be much too flimsy and fragile. It will never last for very long.

NARRATOR: But the first pig would not listen. So he gathered together all the straw he could find and began to build his house. Before too much time had passed, it was completed. He soon moved in.

PIG 2: That's not for me. I shall build my house of wood. It will be a very easy house to build. It will not take much time, and I should be able to complete it in just a few days.

PIG 3: That will never do. It takes time and hard work to build a house that can withstand the rain and wind. Not only must a house withstand the weather, it should also be able to protect us from the wolf.

NARRATOR: But the second pig would not listen. So he gathered up all the wood planks he could find and began to build his house. Before too much time had passed, it was completed. He soon moved in.

PIG 3: That's not for me. I shall build my house of bricks. It will take lots of work and lots of time. But I will have a sturdy house. I will have a house that will protect me from the weather. But most important, I will have a house that can protect me from the wolf.

NARRATOR: So the third pig gathered all the bricks he could find and began to build his house. The building took a long time, and the third pig put lots of work into his house. While the other two pigs were playing and singing and laughing, the third pig worked hard at building his house out of bricks. Finally, after much time, the house was finished and the third pig moved in.

A few days later, while out walking along the road, the third pig saw the tracks of a big wolf. He rushed home. Before too long, the wolf came up the road—right up to the first pig's house.

WOLF: Come out, come out. I want to speak with you.

PIG 1:	I would rather stay where I am.
WOLF:	OK, then I'll make you come out.
NARRATOR:	With that, the wolf took a very large breath and blew with all his might. All the straw of the first pig's house blew away. The first pig, filled with fear, slipped through the straw, out the back, and ran to the second pig's house.
WOLF:	[angrily] Come back, come back!
NARRATOR:	The wolf scampered over to the second pig's house. Both the first pig and the second pig leaned against the door so that the wolf wouldn't be able to blow it down.
PIG 2:	I hope this house won't fall down. I hope it is strong enough to withstand the wolf's breath.
WOLF:	Open up, open up! I want to speak with you.
NARRATOR:	The two pigs held fast to the door. They were very scared of what might happen. The wolf stood just outside the door and filled his lungs with an enormous breath. Suddenly, with a giant blow the entire house collapsed, just like a pack of cards.

Fortunately the third pig was watching what was happening. He opened the door to his house and shouted to his brothers: |
| **PIG 3:** | Come here, come here quickly! |
| **NARRATOR:** | With that, the first and second pigs scrambled over to their brother's brick house, dashed through the door, and quickly bolted it against the wolf. The wolf was close behind them, but the door slammed in his face. He was very angry, and he gathered all the air he could into his lungs. With a might huff and a mighty puff he blew against the third pig's door. But the house did not budge an inch. Again and again, the wolf blew against the house. And again and again, the house did not move. |

83

Exhausted, the wolf leaned against the house to rest. It was then that he saw a ladder leaning against the side of the house. He decided to play a trick on the three pigs and quickly climbed the ladder to the roof.

PIG 1: Look, brothers. The wolf is climbing onto the roof.

PIG 2: Yes, he thinks he can trick us. But I think we are much smarter now.

PIG 3: Yes, my brothers, let's build a fire in the fireplace.

NARRATOR: And so the three pigs built a large fire in the fireplace. The wolf, who was now very hungry, began to slide down the chimney. In no time, he landed in the fire. The flames licked his hairy coat, and soon his tail was on fire.

WOLF: Ouch, ouch! Help, help! My tail is on fire! My tail is on fire!

PIG 1: You get what you deserve.

PIG 2: We hope you've learned your lesson.

PIG 3: Be gone, evil wolf, be gone.

NARRATOR: And with that, the wolf ran out the door, his tail still on fire.

WOLF: Never again. Never again will I go down a chimney.

NARRATOR: The wolf ran as fast as he could down the road and straight toward the river. The three pigs danced and sang with joy. And the wolf never bothered them again.

The Ugly Duckling

STAGING: Place all the characters behind music stands or lecterns. The ugly duckling may wish to hold his or her script and walk across the staging area, having conversations with each of the other characters.

Narrator 1				Narrator 2
X				X
		Ugly Duckling		
		X		
Mother Duck	Bird	Old Woman	Farmer	Young Swan
X	X	X	X	X

NARRATOR 1: Once upon a time in a far off country there lived a duck family on an old farm. The mother duck had been sitting on a clutch of eggs for a long time. One fine morning the eggs hatched, and out popped six very noisy ducklings.

NARRATOR 2: However, one egg was quite a bit bigger than the other eggs. And it didn't hatch at the same time as the other eggs. The mother duck couldn't remember laying a seventh egg.

From Fairy Tales Readers Theatre by Anthony D. Fredericks. Santa Barbara, CA: Libraries Unlimited. Copyright © 2009.

MOTHER DUCK: Hmmm, I wonder where that extra egg came from. I was sure that I laid just six eggs. I wonder if I counted wrong. Hmmm.

NARRATOR 1: The mother duck didn't have a lot of time to think about that, because at last the seventh egg began to hatch. Cra-a-a-ck! Finally the egg cracked open.

NARRATOR 2: Out crawled a large and very strange looking duckling. Gray feathers covered its body. Its head was much larger than its brothers and sisters. It made strange noises.

MOTHER DUCK: I don't understand how this duck could be one of mine. It doesn't look like all the others, and it doesn't sound like all the others. And it's not very pretty like all the others.

NARRATOR 1: It was certain that the new duck didn't look anything like the other ducklings. He grew faster than the others. He ate more than the others. And he took up more room than the others.

NARRATOR 2: As the days went by, the ugly duckling was becoming more and more unhappy. Nobody wanted to play with him, and all the other ducks in the barnyard just laughed at him when he went by. He felt very sad and very lonely.

MOTHER DUCK: I don't understand why he is so different.

NARRATOR 1: The ugly duckling felt worse and worse every day. He cried at night and he cried during the day. He felt as if nobody wanted him.

UGLY DUCKLING: [sadly] Nobody loves me! Nobody wants me! Why am I so different from all the others?

NARRATOR 2: Then one day the ugly duckling decided to run away from the barnyard. Along the way he stopped at a pond. He wanted to question the other birds.

UGLY DUCKLING: Do you know of any ducklings with gray feathers like mine?

BIRD: No, I don't. I've never seen a duckling like you before. You look really strange. You're just an ugly duckling!

NARRATOR 1: The ugly duckling was sadder than before. He didn't understand why he was different from all the other ducklings. He didn't understand why he was such an ugly duckling.

NARRATOR 2: One day as the ugly duckling was walking through the fields, he came upon an old cottage by the side of the road. Inside lived an old woman with very bad eyesight. When she saw the ugly duckling, she decided to catch him.

OLD WOMAN: Now I've got you. I hope that you are a female so that you will lay lots of eggs.

NARRATOR 1: But because the ugly duckling was a male, he laid not a single egg.

OLD WOMAN: You ugly duckling. You ugly, ugly duckling! If you won't lay any eggs for me, then I'll just have to fatten you up and have you for dinner.

NARRATOR 2: The ugly duckling was getting scared. He was so scared that he couldn't even eat. He was getting skinnier and skinnier. Pretty soon he was so skinny that he was able to slip out of his cage and escape on down the road.

UGLY DUCKLING: Oh, woe is me! Nobody loves me! Nobody likes me! All they want to do is make fun of me or capture me or even eat me for dinner. I don't have any friends.

NARRATOR 1: After walking for a long distance, the ugly duckling found himself in a thick bed of reeds beside a lake.

UGLY DUCKLING: I think I'll just stay here. There's plenty of food, and nobody can see me here. I can hide out here forever.

NARRATOR 2: One day at sunset, the ugly duckling heard a noise. He looked up in the sky and saw a flock of beautiful birds flying overhead. Their feathers were white, their beaks were yellow, their necks were long and slender, and they had large, graceful wings.

UGLY DUCKLING: I wish I could look just like them, if only for a day.

NARRATOR 1: Winter came to the country, and the lake began to freeze over. The ugly duckling needed some food, so he set off down the road.

NARRATOR 2: But the road was covered in snow, and it was very difficult for the ugly duckling to walk. Finally he could walk no further, and he fell exhausted on the ground.

FARMER: Well, well, what do we have here? You poor thing—you're almost frozen to death. I'll put you in my pocket and take you home to my children. They'll take good care of you.

NARRATOR 1: In the farmhouse the ugly duckling was showered with care. He was warm, and he always had plenty to eat.

NARRATOR 2: However, by the time spring rolled around the ugly duckling was way too big.

FARMER: I should set him free. He is strong now and can find his own food.

NARRATOR 1: And so the farmer took the ugly duckling to the pond and set him free.

NARRATOR 2: It was then that the duckling saw himself mirrored in the waters of the pond.

UGLY DUCKLING: Goodness, look how I've changed! I can hardly recognize myself any more. I'm no longer ugly.

NARRATOR 1: Right then a flock of swans, winging their way northward after a long winter, swooped down onto the lake.

NARRATOR 2: When the duckling saw them, he realized that he was one of them. He wasn't an ugly duckling after all . . . he was a swan.

YOUNG SWAN: You are a swan—just like us. You now have long white feathers and a yellow beak. You now have a long, graceful neck. Where have you been hiding?

UGLY DUCKLING: It's a long story. It's a long, long story.

NARRATOR 1: Now he swam proudly with all the other swans.

NARRATOR 2: One day, while gliding across the pond, he heard some children talking.

NARRATOR 1: The children said that the new swan was the most beautiful bird they had ever seen.

NARRATOR 2: And the new young swan was filled with happiness!

The Three Billy Goats Gruff

STAGING: The characters may all be standing behind music stands. Or to add a little movement, you may have the three billy goats walk across an imaginary "bridge" (between two sets of chairs placed parallel to each other in the middle of the staging area).

Narrator			Off-stage sound →
X			X →
	Small Billy Goat	Medium Billy Goat	Large Billy Goat
	X	X	X
			Troll
			X

NARRATOR: Once upon a time there were three billy goats who lived in a barn down in the valley. When the snows melted in the spring, they longed to travel up into the mountains to eat the sweet grass that grew there. On their way to the mountains they had to cross over a rushing river. There was a bridge across the river—a bridge made of rickety wooden planks. And underneath the bridge there lived an ugly, one-eyed, and very terrible troll. Before anyone

 From *Fairy Tales Readers Theatre* by Anthony D. Fredericks. Santa Barbara, CA: Libraries Unlimited. Copyright © 2009.

could cross the bridge, they had to get permission from the ugly, one-eyed, and terrible troll. He never gave permission—he just ate anyone who happened to come along.

Well, one day the three billy goats gruff decided that they weren't afraid of the troll. Besides, the green grass was long and sweet, and they wanted some. So they walked up the valley and came to the bridge across the river. The small billy goat was the first one to reach the bridge. He began to walk across.

OFF-STAGE SOUND: Trip, trap. Trip, trap. Trip, trap.

TROLL: [growling] Who's that trotting over my bridge?

SMALL BILLY GOAT: [in a squeaky voice] It's only me. I'm going up to the mountain to eat the sweet grass.

TROLL: [angrily] Oh, no, you're not! I'm going to eat you for breakfast!

SMALL BILLY GOAT: [pleading] Oh, please don't, Mr. Troll. I'm only the smallest billy goat. I'm much too tiny for you to eat. And besides, I wouldn't taste very good. Why don't you wait for my brother, the second billy goat gruff? He's much bigger than me, and he would be much more tasty.

NARRATOR: The troll thought about that for a while and decided that he didn't want to waste his time on such a little goat—especially if there was a bigger goat coming along.

TROLL: All right. You can cross my bridge. Go and eat all the grass you want. Besides, you'll be fatter, and I can eat you when you return.

NARRATOR: So the smallest billy goat crossed the bridge and ran across to the other side.

The troll did not have to wait long for the second billy goat.

OFF-STAGE SOUND: Clip, clop. Clip, clop. Clip, clop.

91

TROLL: [growling] Who's that clattering across my bridge?

MEDIUM BILLY GOAT: It's just me. I'm going up to the mountain to eat some sweet spring grass

TROLL: [angrily] Oh, no, you're not. I'm going to eat you for breakfast.

MEDIUM BILLY GOAT: Oh, please don't. I may be bigger than the first billy goat, but I'm much smaller than my brother, the third billy goat. Why don't you wait for him? He would be a much better meal than me.

NARRATOR: The troll was getting hungrier . . . very hungry. But he did not want to waste his appetite on a middle-sized goat—especially if there was a much larger goat coming along.

TROLL: [gruffly] All right. You can cross my bridge. Go get nice and fat on the mountain, and I'll eat you on your way back.

NARRATOR: So the medium billy goat scampered over the bridge to the other side.

Very soon thereafter, the third billy goat began to cross the bridge.

OFF-STAGE SOUND: Tromp, trap. Tromp, trap. Tromp, trap.

TROLL: [growling] Who's that stomping over my bridge?

LARGE BILLY GOAT: [in a deep voice] It's just me. I'm going up to the mountain to eat the sweet spring grass.

TROLL: [angrily] Oh, no, you're not! I'm going to eat you for breakfast!

LARGE BILLY GOAT: That's what you think!

NARRATOR: The large billy goat lowered his horns, galloped across the bridge, and butted the ugly, one-eyed, terrible troll. Up, up, up went the troll into the air. And then, down, down, down he went into the rushing water of the river below. Soon he disappeared into the swirling waters and was gone forever.

LARGE BILLY GOAT: Now it's time for breakfast.

NARRATOR: The large billy goat walked across the bridge and joined his two brothers on the other side. They spent the rest of the morning enjoying the sweet spring grass in the high mountains.

ALL GOATS: Chomp, chomp, chomp!

Sleeping Beauty

STAGING: All the characters may be seated on tall stools or chairs. Each character should have a music stand or lectern with a copy of the script on it.

	King	Queen	Princess	Witch	Prince	
	X	X	X	X	X	
Narrator 1						Narrator 2
X						X

NARRATOR 1: A long, long time ago there lived a king and queen who, more than anything else, wanted a child. One day, while the queen was bathing in the castle pond, a small frog crawled up next to her. He told her that in just a year's time, she would have her child—a daughter of great beauty.

NARRATOR 2: The frog had spoken the truth, for in a year's time the queen gave birth to a beautiful daughter. The king and queen were both filled with joy and ordered a great feast and a great celebration to honor the birth of their new daughter.

KING:	Let us celebrate! Let us dance! Let us sing! For we have been blessed with a beautiful daughter!
QUEEN:	Yes, this is a joyous day. Let us make merry. And let the bells toll across the kingdom.
NARRATOR 1:	Invitations were sent out across the kingdom, inviting all to come to the festivities. However, one woman, a witch by trade, did not receive an invitation, because she lived in a far corner of the kingdom—a corner not known to the king's messengers.
NARRATOR 2:	And so it was. The celebration took place. There was dancing and there was singing, and there was great merriment. And each of the guests brought a gift for the new child. One by one, they came and laid their gifts at the foot of the baby's cradle. And one by one, they celebrated the birth of the new child.
NARRATOR 1:	But unseen by everyone, the witch had crept into the castle. Suddenly she swept into the Great Hall and yelled at all the guests.
WITCH:	[loudly and angrily] I guess I am not good enough for you. I guess I am not good enough to be invited to your little celebration. And so the die is cast. Because you all have such hard hearts, I, too, have a hard heart. I shall cast a spell on this new child. In her fifteenth year, the daughter of the king and queen shall prick herself on a spindle and shall never wake up. Indeed, she will remain asleep for one hundred years. One hundred years! ONE HUNDRED YEARS SHALL SHE SLEEP!!
NARRATOR 2:	Everyone was shocked at the witch's pronouncement—so much so that a great silence fell over the hall. It was then that the king made a royal command.

KING: I command that every spindle in the kingdom be burned immediately. Every one! Every one must be destroyed!

NARRATOR 1: And so it was. Every spindle in the kingdom was immediately destroyed. There was not a single one to be found anywhere.

NARRATOR 2: Now it came to pass that the young girl grew up. She was both fair and beautiful. She was admired by all who visited the castle as a wise and modest young lady.

NARRATOR 1: Now it came to the time in her life when the young princess was 15 years old. And on that day her father and mother were away. The young maiden, filled with curiosity, went from room to room in the castle, searching for something to do.

NARRATOR 2: At last she came to an old tower in a far corner of the castle. She climbed the winding staircase, and there at the top was a wooden door. She pushed open the door and there, inside a tiny room, was an old woman with a spindle. She was spinning long strands of flax.

PRINCESS: Good day, old woman. And what are you doing in this old tower?

WITCH: Why, I am spinning. I am spinning this beautiful flax.

PRINCESS: And what is that spinning around so merrily?

WITCH: Come. Come and see for yourself.

NARRATOR 1: The young girl reached out. She had scarcely touched the spindle when she pricked her finger. The evil spell fell upon her immediately, and she collapsed into a deep, deep sleep.

NARRATOR 2: Indeed, the spell fell upon the whole of the castle. The king and queen, who had just returned from their journey, fell fast asleep. The whole of the court fell into a great trance. All the king's horses and all the queen's dogs fell into a great slumber. The birds on the roof, the sheep in the stable, the chickens in the yard, the cooks, the butlers, and the stable boys all fell fast, fast asleep. The wind was stilled, and not a leaf moved on any of the trees surrounding the castle.

NARRATOR 1: Around the castle there grew a great hedge of thorns. The hedge grew higher and higher—up and over the castle—until nothing of the castle could be seen. Indeed, the castle disappeared under the great covering of thorns.

NARRATOR 2: But the story of the princess spread far across the land. And from time to time young men would come to the castle to try to pierce the thorny exterior and find the sleeping princess. But each one who tried was caught fast by the thorns and died a most miserable death.

NARRATOR 1: After many, many years a young prince, who had also heard the story, came into the kingdom.

PRINCE: I know that within that thorny hedge and within that hidden castle there sleeps a beautiful maiden—Sleeping Beauty. Although she and the entire court have been asleep for one hundred years, I will go and see my Sleeping Beauty. I am not afraid!

NARRATOR 2: Now, it was the time when the hundred years had passed. It was the time when Sleeping Beauty awoke after her long, long sleep.

NARRATOR 1: When the prince came up to the castle, he saw that it was covered, not by a solid hedge of thorns, but by garlands of beautiful flowers. He entered the castle and saw before him all the sleeping servants, all the sleeping animals, all the castle life still fast asleep where they had fallen one hundred years before.

NARRATOR 2: At last he came to the old tower. As he opened the door at the top, he could see Sleeping Beauty on the floor. Slowly he walked over to her, bent over her, and gave her a kiss. As soon as he kissed her, she awoke from her hundred-year sleep.

PRINCESS: Who are you?

PRINCE: You have been awakened from your deep sleep.

PRINCESS: How long was I asleep?

PRINCE: You were put under a spell by an evil witch and have been asleep for one hundred years.

NARRATOR 1: Then, hand in hand, the prince and the princess walked back down the staircase and into the castle. And at that moment all the animals, all the servants, the king and queen, and all who had fallen sleep were awakened. And once again, the castle was filled with joy and laughter.

NARRATOR 2: And it came to pass that the prince and princess were married in a great celebration. And they lived very happily for the rest of their years.

Cinderella

STAGING: The two narrators should be placed at the rear of the staging area. Each should be standing behind a music stand or lectern. The other characters may be seated on tall stools or chairs. If one is available, you may wish to place a pumpkin (or a papier-mâché replica) in the middle of the staging area.

```
Narrator 1                                              Narrator 2
   X                                                        X


                    Stepsister 1        Stepsister 2
                         X                   X
      Cinderella
         X
              Fairy                   Prince
               X                        X
```

NARRATOR 1: Once upon a time there lived a beautiful young maiden who was very unhappy. He mother had died, and her father had married an evil woman with two equally evil daughters. The stepmother and the two stepsisters made the young girl, whose name was Cinderella, work hard all day long—from morning until night.

NARRATOR 2: She had to scrub the floors, wash the dishes, cook the meals, and wear dirty, hand-me-down clothes all day long. She was always picked on and was always yelled at.

STEPSISTER 1: [commandingly] Cinderella, wash these floors. Come, and wash these floors right now!

STEPSISTER 2: [commandingly] Cinderella, come and cook me my dinner. I am very hungry, and I want my dinner right now.

STEPSISTER 1: [commandingly] Cinderella, come and clean the pots and pans. They are dirty and need cleaning right now.

STEPSISTER 2: [commandingly] Cinderella, you are lazy. You are lazy, lazy, lazy. Come and do some work you lazy, lazy girl!

NARRATOR 1: One day, some very lovely and very beautiful dresses arrived at the house. There was a ball to be held at the castle—a ball in honor of the prince, who had recently returned from a very long journey.

NARRATOR 2: Unfortunately the dresses were only for the stepmother and her two daughters. There was not a dress for Cinderella.

STEPSISTER 1: [gloating] Ha, Cinderella, there is not a dress for you. You must stay here while we go to the ball and dance with the handsome prince.

STEPSISTER 2: [gloating] Yes, you must stay here and scrub the floors and wash the dishes and do all the work while we are dancing at the castle with the prince.

CINDERELLA: [sadly] Oh, I am so sad. All I do is work, work, work. I wish that just once I could go to the ball at the castle and dance through the night—just like everyone else.

NARRATOR 1: Just then there was a flash of light in the kitchen.

NARRATOR 2: Just then a small fairy appeared in the kitchen.

FAIRY: Do not be afraid, Cinderella. I can grant you your wishes. You shall go to the ball and dance with the handsome prince.

CINDERELLA: But how can I? All I have are these dirty rags. Surely the prince's guards will turn me away from the door when they see how I am dressed.

FAIRY: Do not fear—for there is magic in the air.

NARRATOR 1: And with that, the fairy flicked her magic wand. In the twinkling of an eye, Cinderella was dressed in the most beautiful gown of all; indeed, many would say that it was the prettiest dress in the entire kingdom.

NARRATOR 2: She was wearing gold rings and a lovely pearl necklace. Her hair was hanging in long, golden braids. She was, indeed, a most beautiful woman.

FAIRY: Now, you will need something to get you to the ball. Bring me a pumpkin.

CINDERELLA: At once!

NARRATOR 1: Cinderella ran to the cellar and fetched a large pumpkin.

FAIRY: Now we need six mice.

NARRATOR 2: Cinderella ran to the cupboard, and there huddled in the corner were six tiny mice.

FAIRY: This is all good.

NARRATOR 1: The fairy once again flicked her magic wand, and the pumpkin turned into a sparkling coach.

NARRATOR 2: Then the fairy flicked her magic wand again, and the six mice turned into large white horses.

CINDERELLA: I cannot believe my eyes! This is too wonderful for words.

FAIRY: Listen, oh beautiful Cinderella. You will now be presented to the court of the handsome prince—a handsome prince who will be enchanted by your loveliness. But you must remember this—you must leave the ball at midnight and come straight home. For at midnight the spell will be broken. Your coach will turn back into a pumpkin, your six horses will turn back into mice, and you will be dressed, once again, in dirty old rags. Do you understand, Cinderella?

CINDERELLA: Yes, I understand!

NARRATOR 1: When Cinderella entered the ballroom at the castle, everyone stopped what they were doing to look at the beautiful maiden. "Who is she?" they asked.

NARRATOR 2: When the prince saw Cinderella, he was overcome by her beauty. He walked over to her and asked her dance. And the two of them danced all through the night.

STEPSISTER 1: [angrily] Who is that woman? Who does she think she is?

STEPSISTER 2: [angrily] Yes, who is she, and where did she come from? It seems the prince only has eyes for her.

PRINCE: [to Cinderella] You are the most beautiful woman I have ever seen.

CINDERELLA: Thank you, dear prince. But in a short time I shall be gone. I shall be gone—never more to be seen again.

PRINCE: What do you mean?

CINDERELLA: It is true. Soon I must depart this palace and return to whence I came.

NARRATOR 1: Cinderella had a wonderful time at the ball. But all of a sudden she heard the sound of the town clock . . . it was the first stroke of midnight.

NARRATOR 2: Cinderella remembered what the fairy had told her. Without a word of good-bye, she slipped from the prince's arms and ran down the castle steps.

NARRATOR 1: As she ran, she lost one of her slippers, but she had no time to stop and pick it up. She had to return home before the last stroke of midnight.

NARRATOR 2: The prince, who was now madly in love with the beautiful maiden, scooped up the slipper.

PRINCE: [commandingly] Everyone, you must go and search for the girl whose foot this slipper fits. I will never be happy again until she is found.

NARRATOR 1: The prince's ministers searched high and low and tried the slipper on the foot of every woman they met along the way.

NARRATOR 2: Arriving at the house where Cinderella lived, they tried the slipper on her stepmother and her two stepsisters, but it did not fit any of them.

NARRATOR 1: Finally they tried the slipper on Cinderella's foot . . .

NARRATOR 2: . . . and it fit just right.

STEPSISTER 1: How can it fit her? She is so ugly and only wears dirty rags.

STEPSISTER 2: Yes, how can she be the one? This is not right!

FAIRY: I will show you who she really is!

NARRATOR 1: And the fairy waved her magic wand . . .

NARRATOR 2: . . . and Cinderella appeared in a splendid dress, with golden hair and the finest jewels.

CINDERELLA: I can't believe it! I just can't believe it!

PRINCE: She is, indeed, the most beautiful woman in the land. And I shall make her my wife.

NARRATOR 1: And so it was that the prince and Cinderella were married in a grand ceremony, and they lived all their days in great happiness.

NARRATOR 2: Meanwhile, the two stepsisters spent the rest of their days scrubbing the floors, washing the dishes, and cleaning the house . . . all in their dirty rags, of course.

PART III

FAIRY TALES (WITH A TOUCH OF HUMOR)

Beauty and This Incredibly Ugly Guy

STAGING: Narrator 1 may stand to the left of the staging area; Narrator 2 may stand to the right. The two characters may be seated on high stools or chairs in the center. They may wish to use plastic toy phones as props.

	Ugly Guy X		Beauty X	
Narrator 1 X				Narrator 2 X

NARRATOR 1: [rambling and rapidly] Once upon a time there was this deep dark forest in which there was a little cottage where this man and this woman lived with all their children, and all the animals of the forest would be their friends, and they ate berries and leaves and everyone was happy and smiling and just wanted to be left alone so they could eventually live happily ever after, except for the fact that these out-of-work storytellers came wandering through the forest one day and decided to turn the family's life into some incredibly neat fairy tale or fable or

legend or something like that so that they would all become incredibly rich and be able to live happily ever after for the rest of their lives, but do you think they even thought of sharing all their riches with that family deep in the enchanted forest? No, of course they didn't, but that's probably another story, which I don't have time to tell you because I'm trying to tell you this story that really isn't a real story but just a story I made up because I wanted to get rich and famous like all those other storytellers; so what I did was take one of their stories—actually I just borrowed it for a while—and decided to change just a couple of the facts and events; well, maybe I changed a lot of the facts and events, so that I could tell it to you all and you all would become incredibly excited and want to hear it again and again and want to tell your friends about this story, and they would want to hear it again and again and, of course, I would become very rich and very famous and invite you all over to my castle and give you a ride in my incredibly fast carriage; but maybe I'm getting ahead of myself; perhaps I'd better just tell you the story and see if you like it first—OK, OK, OK? Well, anyway, here goes!

[more slowly] Once upon a time there was this really gorgeous looking blond maiden; I mean a real knock-out, a real beauty, with a fantastic personality and everything. As you might expect, all the princes from the local castle wanted to date her and take her to the movies, and concerts, and all the other kinds of things guys do with incredibly beautiful maidens. But this incredibly ravishing young maiden didn't like all the young men in the castle, most of whom were about as stupid as a doormat anyway. Well, it just so happened that there was this really ugly guy over in the next castle. I mean, you talk about ugly; he was so bad he made paint peel just by being in a room. He was so ugly he had to put a bag over his head just to sneak up on a glass of water to take a drink. He was so ugly that dogs would howl whenever he walked by. He was so ugly . . . .

NARRATOR 2: Will you just get on with the story, already?

NARRATOR 1: OK, OK. So anyway, this really really really ugly guy wants to take the fantastically stunning young maiden out for a date. So he calls her up one evening.

UGLY GUY: Good evening, may I please speak to the phenomenally stunning young maiden, please? [pause] Thank you.

UGLY GUY: Hello, wonderfully gorgeous young maiden. This is an incredibly ugly guy.

BEAUTY: Oh, hello. Don't you sit behind me in math class?

UGLY GUY: Yeah, that's me. I thought you never noticed me.

BEAUTY: Well, actually, I haven't. It's just that all the other girls have been talkin' about you. So what do you want?

UGLY GUY: [shyly] Wel-l-l-l-l-l-l-l-l. You see. The Fall Ball is coming up in a few weeks down at the castle. And I was just sorta, kinda, well you see I was just thinking and wondering and maybe even kinda hopin' that . . . well, would you like to go with me to the ball?

BEAUTY: Are you asking me for a date?

UGLY GUY: [unsure and rambling] Well, yes I am. Would you like to go with me? I mean I realize that I'm certainly one of the ugliest and strangest and most repulsive creatures you've ever seen. And I'm probably not a very good dancer or anything like that. And I can barely carry on a conversation with anyone. And sometimes I have bad breath and really gross people out when I talk with them. And I'm sorta clumsy and will probably spill punch and cookies all over you. And I never take a bath and probably smell like I've been living in a sewer all

109

my life. And I never comb my hair or brush my teeth. And my clothes are all dirty and torn and beat up and ragged and stained and all that stuff. And I never clip my toenails or wash my socks. But in spite of all that, I've got a really great personality.

BEAUTY: Well, you know, I am sort of intrigued. I've never really gone out with an extraordinarily grotesque and hideous guy before. It sounds like it might be fun. OK, yeah, sure, why not? Let's go out.

UGLY GUY: [excitedly] Oh, wow! That's great. Look, why don't I pick you up in my beat-up old hay wagon next Friday night at about 7:00? OK?

BEAUTY: That sounds good. I'll see you then.

NARRATOR 2: And so it was that this remarkably repulsive and unattractive guy was able to take the most incredibly ravishing and stunning maiden in the whole kingdom to the annual Fall Ball. And of course they had a great time . . . except for that time the really monstrous and unsightly guy tried to kiss the wonderfully and exquisitely beautiful young maiden. But that's another story.

Adapted from Anthony D. Fredericks, *Frantic Frogs and Other Frankly Fractured Folktales for Readers Theatre* (Westport, CT: Teacher Ideas Press, 1993).

Coughy: The Dwarf Snow White Never Told You About

STAGING: The narrator should sit on a high stool in the front center of the staging area. The other characters may stand, or sit on stools.

	Doc	Dopey	Sleepy
	X	X	X
	Grumpy	Sneezy	
	X	X	
Narrator			
X			

NARRATOR: [sometimes rambling] Now, you know how these stories go. See, there's this "once upon a time" part of the story that tells you when and where the story took place. Then there's this little ditty about some wonderfully beautiful princess, and some incredible hunk of a prince, who meet each other, are separated by some ragged old witch or a wicked wizard with an attitude problem, and then by the end of the story are reunited again to live happily ever after. After you've heard one, haven't you just about heard them all? Think about it, just how many beautiful princesses and handsome princes are there? I mean, look at me . . . I'm good lookin', handsome, bright, intelligent, and so-o-o-o-o-o incredibly smart, but do you see me putting on some green leotards to go prancing around some deep dark forest to look for some drop-dead princess who wants to be rescued from an evil spell? Come on, let's get real! I've sure got better things to do with my time. But anyway, on with this story, which is a story about this girl who just happens to find herself in the midst of a deep dark forest, having been put there by her evil (what else?) stepmother. She's obviously lost and alone and frightened and cold and all that other stuff when she just happens to come upon a small cottage in the middle of the woods (how convenient). So she walks in, finds nobody home, and decides to pick up a broom and clean out the place (just like they do in all those other stories). Anyway, she is polishing the silverware and scrubbing the floors when the real occupants of the house come home from work. They're small, tiny, short, and undersized little men—that's right, you guessed it, the seven dwarfs. Except in this story there's another little dwarf that was left out of the original story. Of course there's Dopey, and Sneezy, and Doc, and Sleepy, and Grumpy, and Happy, and Bashful. But this new dwarf, his name is Coughy. Why? Well, stupid, it's probably because he coughs a lot. Anyway, let's get on with the story.

SNOW WHITE: [surprised] My goodness, look at you all! How did you all get to be so short?

SNEEZY: [irritated] Look, lady. Just answer this. How did you get in our house, and who invited you here, anyway?

SNOW WHITE: Well, you see, the Narrator said it was OK to just walk in here and start the story from this point.

NARRATOR: Hey, don't look at me, guys. I just work here.

DOC: [defiantly] Yeah, just what makes you think you can just waltz in here any time you like, clean our house, and become an important character in our story? Do you think you're some fancy pants young model who can just do anything she wants and get away with it? Well, I've got news for you, sister. This here's the real "Deep Dark Forest," and we don't allow just any character to crawl into our house any old time she wishes just so she can get a starring role in a story.

DOPEY: [slowly] Yea, just remember what happened to that Goldilocks woman. You heard what she got for that "breaking and entering" episode in the Three Bears house on the other side of the forest. So you'd better just watch yourself, sister!

SLEEPY: [snappy] So what's your story, White? In fact, I bet your last name isn't even White. I bet it's something like "Ball," or "Drift," or "Storm," or something like that. White's probably just a made-up name you use in these stories. Isn't that right?

SNOW WHITE: No really, it's really White, Snow White. You see, I was born one dark morning during the middle of a blinding snowstorm and my father couldn't . . .

GRUMPY: [slightly angry] Look, we've all heard that sad tale before, and believe me, we don't buy it for one second. Who do you think you're foolin'?

DOC: So let's get back to the real issue here. How come you're in our house washing our pots and pans and sweeping our floor? Maybe, just maybe, we happen to like being slobs. Did you ever think about that? What makes you think that just because there's garbage all over our cottage and dust and dirt everywhere, that you have a right to come in and clean it up? We just happen to like living this way. I mean, look at all the boys and girls out in the audience. Aren't their rooms messy and dirty? Don't they have dirty clothes all over the floor and messy beds? Don't they like to live like slobs, too? You're darn right they do! So what are you going to do, visit each and every one of THEIR homes and clean them up? Fat chance!

DOPEY: Yeah, Doc's right. We just happen to like living like pigs. Is there any law against that?

GRUMPY: And that certainly doesn't give you any right to come in here in the middle of a nice lovely story and start all this dust flying around.

SNOW WHITE: Hey, guys, ease up! I was just trying to help. Besides, I thought it might be a nice way to get this story moving along. After all, all the kids in the audience are pretty familiar with the original story, and I thought that this would be a good way to get the new story off the ground. Oh, my gosh! I forgot about the new story. I was supposed to tell them about your cousin Coughy.

DOC: [irritated] Now see what you've gone and done. You've spent so much time on this supposedly great introduction to the story that we're all out of time for the rest of the story. Thanks a lot!!!

NARRATOR: [at times rambling] Well, as it was, Snow White was never able to tell the story about the eighth dwarf, Coughy. But just so you don't feel totally left out, Coughy was later sent to the castle, the one where the evil stepmother lived, to pick up a prescription for his cough. He got a coughing attack just as the evil stepmother was walking by the drugstore, and he coughed all over her. The evil stepmother came down with a case of pneumonia and died a short time later. Coughy became a hero to all the townspeople and eventually had a statue erected in his honor in the center of town. Some talent agency

114

signed him to appear in a TV commercial for a new cold medicine. He eventually wound up making a lot of money and retiring to a condo in Hawaii (which is why you never hear about him in the usual Snow White stories). The other dwarfs have to continue working in the diamond mine to try to earn a living. And Snow White . . . well, she just keeps going through the forest cleaning up all the cottages she can find.

_____

Adapted from Anthony D. Fredericks, *Frantic Frogs and Other Frankly Fractured Folktales for Readers Theatre* (Westport, CT: Teacher Ideas Press, 1993).

Don't Kiss Sleeping Beauty, She's Got Really Bad Breath

STAGING: The narrator stands off to the side. The characters may sit on stools or chairs. Or they may wish to stand in a circle in front of the audience.

Narrator X			
Prince 1 X	Prince 2 X	Prince 3 X	Prince 4 X

NARRATOR: Once upon a time, there was this very beautiful princess. All the princes wanted to marry her. However, one day a wicked witch made this beautiful girl eat a poisoned apple. Beauty (that was her name) fell fast asleep. All the princes knew that it would take a kiss to wake her up.

PRINCE 1: Wow! All I have to do is kiss Sleeping Beauty, and she will awaken from her sleep to be my bride.

NARRATOR: [to the prince] That's right, Prince 1.

NARRATOR: [to the audience] Let's see what happens when Prince 1 returns to the castle to tell his prince friends about his discovery.

PRINCE 1: Hey, guys. You're not going to believe this, but Sleeping Beauty is sound asleep in the enchanted forest. And she is waiting for one of us to give her a kiss that will wake her up.

PRINCE 2: Well, why didn't you kiss her?

PRINCE 1: Well, it seems as she has really bad breath . . . . I mean really bad breath! WHEW! Did it stink!!!

PRINCE 3: You mean, you didn't kiss her after all?

PRINCE 1: No way, José. Her breath was so bad I couldn't even get in the room.

PRINCE 4: That's hard to believe. You mean, her breath is so bad that we can't even get close enough to kiss her? Wow, what a waste!

PRINCE 1: Yeah, and you know what else? She snores like a bear. Every time she breathes the windows rattle and the dishes in the kitchen crack and break.

PRINCE 3: Boy, that's unbelievable!

PRINCE 1: Not only is she stinking up the air, but she's making the whole neighborhood shake with her snoring. Nobody wants to live in the enchanted forest anymore.

PRINCE 2: Well, how are we going to wake her up? Doesn't somebody have to kiss her in order for this story to end the right way?

PRINCE 1: Hey, maybe you, pal, but not me! If you want to go ahead and kiss old "Hog's Breath," then help yourself.

NARRATOR: And so nobody wanted to kiss Sleeping Beauty. She just slept in the forest, making loud noises and stinking up the air. And if you ever go into the forest and listen real hard, you can still hear her today.

Adapted from Anthony D. Fredericks, *Tadpole Tales and Other Totally Terrific Treats for Readers Theatre* (Westport, CT: Teacher Ideas Press, 1997).

Goldilocks and the Three Hamsters

STAGING: The narrator sits off to the side on a tall stool or chair. The other characters may be standing or sitting in chairs.

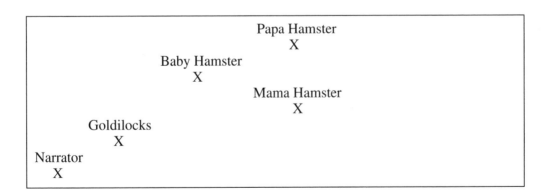

NARRATOR: Once upon a time there were three hamsters. One was Baby Hamster. He was the smallest. The middle-sized hamster was Mama Hamster. The biggest hamster was Papa Hamster. They all lived together in a cage in Mrs. Johnson's classroom. One day Mama Hamster baked some hamster food in the hamster oven and put it on the hamster table for breakfast. They all stood around to eat.

BABY HAMSTER: OWWWW! This hamster food is too hot!

MAMA HAMSTER: You are right, Baby Hamster. What should we do until it is cool?

PAPA HAMSTER: Let's go for a run on the exercise wheel on the other side of the cage. When we come back the hamster food will be just right.

NARRATOR: The hamster family left their hamster breakfast cooling on the hamster table. They walked over to the exercise wheel inside their hamster cage to go for a morning run. While they were on the wheel, a little girl named Goldilocks, who was a student in Mrs. Johnson's class, was walking by the cage. She was on her way to get her pencil sharpened. She walked by the cage and smelled the hamster food.

GOLDILOCKS: OOOHHH. That smells so good! I didn't have anything for breakfast at home. Maybe I'll just take a quick peek inside this cage.

NARRATOR: Goldilocks looked through the bars in the cage and into the little hamster house. She unlocked the cage and stuck her head right inside.

GOLDILOCKS: Look at this big bowl of hamster food. I'll have to try it. Oh, no, this is just too hot. Maybe I'll eat this middle-sized bowl. No, it is just a little too cold. I'll try this tiny bowl. Oh, yes! This is just right!

NARRATOR: Goldilocks ate all the hamster food in Baby Hamster's bowl. Then she began to look around the inside of the little hamster house. She noticed the three hollow tubes that the hamsters played in.

GOLDILOCKS: Look at those tubes. I think I'll stick my finger in the big one first. Goodness! This one's too big. Maybe the middle-sized tube is better. No, it's still too big. I think this little one will be just right.

NARRATOR: But when Goldilocks put her big fat finger inside the tiny little tube, she got stuck. She shook and shook and shook her finger until the tube flew off and smashed into a hundred pieces on the floor. That made her very angry. She decided to look around the house some more. She found the three smelly old rags that the hamsters used for their beds.

GOLDILOCKS: Those smelly old rags sure do look interesting. I think I'll pick them up. I'll try the big one first. Oh, no, this is much too dirty for me. Perhaps the middle-sized one is better. No, this one's much too stinky. I'll try the little one. Yes, this one's not too dirty and not too smelly. I'll use it to blow my nose.

NARRATOR: But when Goldilocks tried to pull her head out of the cage, it became stuck. Soon the three hamsters came back from their exercise wheel.

BABY HAMSTER: Look, Father! Somebody has been in our house.

MAMA HAMSTER: Let's go in very carefully and very slowly.

PAPA HAMSTER: SOMEONE HAS BEEN EATING MY HAMSTER FOOD!

MAMA HAMSTER: SOMEONE HAS BEEN EATING MY HAMSTER FOOD!

BABY HAMSTER: SOMEONE HAS BEEN EATING MY HAMSTER FOOD! And it's all gone!

NARRATOR: The hamsters began looking around the house. Papa Hamster saw that his hollow tube had been moved.

PAPA HAMSTER: SOMEONE HAS BEEN PLAYING WITH MY HOLLOW TUBE!

MAMA HAMSTER: SOMEONE HAS BEEN PLAYING WITH MY HOLLOW TUBE!

BABY HAMSTER: SOMEONE HAS BEEN PLAYING WITH MY HOLLOW TUBE! And they broke it into a thousand pieces.

NARRATOR: The hamsters went to the sleeping area of their house. Papa Hamster was the first to see that his rag had been disturbed.

PAPA HAMSTER: SOMEONE HAS BEEN MESSING WITH MY RAG!

MAMA HAMSTER: SOMEONE HAS BEEN MESSING WITH MY RAG!

BABY HAMSTER: SOMEONE HAS BEEN MESSING WITH MY RAG! And, look, there she is with her head caught in our cage.

NARRATOR: [faster and faster] Goldilocks got very scared. The three hamsters began running toward her. Goldilocks pulled harder and harder. The hamsters were getting closer and closer. Goldilocks was getting more and more scared. Finally, with one last yank, she pulled her head out just in the nick of time. [slowly] After that, she promised she would never ever eat hamster food again. The three hamsters got a large rat to guard their house and put locks on all their doors. And they all lived happily after ever.

Adapted from Anthony D. Fredericks, *Silly Salamanders and Other Slightly Stupid Stuff for Readers Theatre* (Westport, CT: Teacher Ideas Press, 2000).

Little Red Riding Hood Punches the Wolf Character Right in the Kisser

STAGING: The characters may all be seated on tall stools. The narrator may be standing, or seated on a stool, at the edge of the staging area.

Cinderella	Snow White	Sleeping Beauty	Little Red Riding Hood	
X	X	X	X	
				Narrator
				X

NARRATOR: Once upon a time a bunch of storybook characters got together for their monthly literary meeting, where they talked about all the good literature (and some bad literature, too) that was being shared with students in schools all over the country. Well, as often happened, the discussion soon turned to some of the characters our friends here [points] have to deal with every time a story is read aloud.

LITTLE RED RIDING HOOD: [upset] Hey, girls, you know what? I'm getting just a little sick and tired of always packing a little picnic basket full of goodies, skipping through the deep dark woods, and meeting this hairball of a character—whom the writers call a wolf—and then racing him over to Granny's house to see who can get to Granny's bed first.

SLEEPING BEAUTY: Zzzzzzzzzzzzz.

SNOW WHITE: Yeah, you got it tough, sister. Every time some teacher tells that story to her little students, you really get the "short end of the stick," so to speak. I mean, why does your adventure have to have some guy with an attitude problem who hasn't shaved in a month or more?

CINDERELLA: Yeah, who do those writers think they are? How come we females always have to deal with mean, old, or ugly characters all the time? Just look in the library and you'll see what I mean. How many stories do you know that are filled with handsome, polite, and very rich princes? Noooooooo, they're all filled with mean, old, or ugly dudes.

SLEEPING BEAUTY: Zzzzzzzzzzzzz.

LITTLE RED RIDING HOOD: It sure is getting to be a drag. I don't mind packing the picnic basket every time the story is told. I don't even mind taking a stroll through the woods and listening to the sounds of nature. I don't even mind helping out my poor sweet old Granny every once in a while. But when I have to deal with that fur ball with bad breath . . . .

CINDERELLA: He's never been nice to you. He growls at you in the woods. He outraces you to Granny's house. He steals Granny's pajamas and tosses her under the bed. And then he puts his smelly old body in her bed to wait for you to waltz in the door. It's really sickening.

SNOW WHITE: It's ugly, I tell you. Really, really ugly. He smells, he stinks, he never washes, and you have to talk with him every single time some parent or teacher tells the story. Wow, you really have it bad, girl!

SLEEPING BEAUTY: Zzzzzzzzzzz.

LITTLE RED RIDING HOOD: You know what I should do? The next time I see that stinky fur ball, I should just walk right up to him and sock him one right in the kisser. That would teach him a lesson. I bet he'd never mess with me again.

SNOW WHITE: Yeah, right in the kisser. You'd sure show him who was boss!

CINDERELLA: Yeah, just haul off and land one right in the middle of his hairy old wolf face. By the time he woke up, you'd be all the way to Granny's house, and he'd have a headache for at least a week.

LITTLE RED RIDING HOOD: Yeah, I really should teach him a lesson he'd never forget.

SLEEPING BEAUTY: Zzzzzzzzzzz.

CINDERELLA: [defiantly] Besides, you'd show him who was really in charge. Those fancy dancy writers all think that they're all soooooo smart and brilliant. They just sit around all day making up these stories where these ugly wolfy fur balls attack all us good lookin' and very intelligent ladies. Obviously all the writers are males, 'cause women writers would never

125

have some dude with a furry face and bad breath as the lead character in a story. They'd make sure that the women were all princesses and queens and all the furry males would be kept in a cage in the dungeon of some faraway castle . . . or something like that.

SNOW WHITE: Hey, I tell you what. Why don't we all get together, march right down to that deep, dark forest that Red has to walk through in every story, and teach that fur ball of a wolf a real lesson? What do you say?

SLEEPING BEAUTY: Zzzzzzzzzzzzz.

CINDERELLA: Yeah, that sounds like a great idea!

LITTLE RED RIDING HOOD: I'm all for it. Let's go.

NARRATOR: And so it was that our three heroines (nobody could wake up Sleeping Beauty) marched out of Red Riding Hood's house and into the forest. Before too long they were able to locate the wolf, who was dozing under a tree and waiting for the next story to begin. The three women surrounded the wolf and watched as Red Riding Hood punched him right in the kisser. I mean she really socked him good! Wham! Blam!! He never stood a chance. He literally staggered out of Red Riding Hood's story and into another story, about some giant guy who lived at the top of a very tall vegetable. But all he could do in that story was mumble a lot and walk around in circles. He was never the same again. In his place, Red Riding Hood hired a cute little bunny and completely rewrote the ending of her story. And of course she lived happily ever after.

SLEEPING BEAUTY: Zzzzzzzzzzzzz.

Adapted from Anthony D. Fredericks, _MORE_ _Frantic Frogs and Other Frankly Fractured Folktales for Readers Theatre_ (Westport, CT: Teacher Ideas Press, 2008).

The Gingerbread Boy Gets Baked at 350° for 15–20 Minutes

STAGING: The narrator may stand off to the side. The other characters may sit on tall stools or in chairs.

Narrator		Gingerbread Boy		
X		X		
	Little Old Woman		Little Old Man	
	X		X	

NARRATOR: Once upon a time there was a Little Old Woman and a Little Old Man. They lived alone in a little old house in the middle of a little old forest in a little old country in a little old time. One day the Little Old Woman decided to make a little old Gingerbread Boy. I don't know, maybe she was thinking that the Gingerbread Boy would become her son one day. But how a Gingerbread Boy could become the son of a Little Old Woman and a Little Old Man is something that I just don't understand. Hey, I'm just the narrator, not some rocket scientist! Anyway, let's just say that the Little Old Woman was just a little touched in the head—what you and I might call crazy. Anyway, on with our story.

LITTLE OLD WOMAN: Well, now I'm finished mixing the flour, butter, sugar, ginger, and all those other ingredients. I think I'll just shape them all into a little Gingerbread Boy. Won't that be cute!

LITTLE OLD MAN: Hey, Little Old Woman, why are you doing that?

LITTLE OLD WOMAN: Because we don't have a son of our own, my Little Old Man.

LITTLE OLD MAN: [aside to the audience] I think the narrator person is right. I think my Little Old Woman is just slightly crazy. But what do I know? Anyway, that's just the way she is, so let's just get on with the story.

LITTLE OLD WOMAN: Never mind what that silly narrator said. I'm just going to put this little Gingerbread Boy into the oven and bake him for about 15 to 20 minutes at a temperature of 350°. Then maybe we'll eat him up for dinner.

LITTLE OLD MAN: Whoa there, my loving Little Old Woman. Why would you want to eat up the Gingerbread Boy for dinner? Didn't you just say that maybe he could be our son.

LITTLE OLD WOMAN: Yeah, I did. Sometimes I get confused and don't know what I'm talking about. I guess I just can't make up my mind. I don't know if I really want something to eat for dinner or whether I just want to have a son.

LITTLE OLD MAN: Well, a gingerbread son would be nice. He could mow the lawn. He could wash the windows. He could sweep the driveway. He could do lots of things around here. After all, Little Old Woman, both you and I are old and little, and we can't do all the things we used to.

128

LITTLE OLD WOMAN: You are right, my Little Old Man. But I'm really getting very hungry. I haven't had anything to eat for a long time. And, just like our friend, Old Mother Hubbard, we don't have anything in the cupboard.

LITTLE OLD MAN: Yes, you're right. There's very little to eat around this little house. Maybe we should just forget about having a gingerbread son and just eat him up as soon as he gets out of the oven.

NARRATOR: All the time the Little Old Woman and the Little Old Man were talking, the little Gingerbread Boy was in the oven baking away at 350°. But he was also listening very carefully to the conversation the Little Old Man and the Little Old Woman were having. And to tell the truth, he didn't like what he was hearing. He decided that this wasn't the place where he wanted to live. So, while the Little Old Man and the Little Old Woman were talking away, the Gingerbread Boy snuck out of the oven, tip-toed across the kitchen floor, and slipped out the back door.

LITTLE OLD WOMAN: [confused] Hey, where did our Gingerbread Boy go?

LITTLE OLD MAN: Why did he run away from us?

NARRATOR: Well, to tell the truth, the Gingerbread Boy wanted to save his skin, so to speak. But he quickly discovered that life outside a 350° oven can be quite dangerous, especially when there's a fox around. He wound up having more adventures than he was ready for . . . and some of them weren't very pretty. But then again, that's another story. So now it's time to say good-bye.

LITTLE OLD MAN: [waving] Good-bye.

LITTLE OLD WOMAN: [waving] Good-bye.

LITTLE OLD MAN: [whispering to the Little Old Woman] Say, I'm still hungry. What have we got around here to eat?

Adapted from Anthony D. Fredericks, *MORE Frantic Frogs and Other Frankly Fractured Folktales for Readers Theatre* (Westport, CT: Teacher Ideas Press, 2008).

References

Cunningham, P., and R. Allington. 2003. *Classrooms That Work: They Can All Read and Write.* Boston: Allyn & Bacon.

Dixon, N., A. Davies, and C. Politano. 1996. *Learning with Readers Theatre: Building Connections.* Winnipeg, MB: Peguis Publishers.

Fredericks, A. D. 1993. *Frantic Frogs and Other Frankly Fractured Folktales for Readers Theatre.* Westport, CT: Teacher Ideas Press.

———. 2001. *Guided Reading for Grades 3–6.* Austin, TX: Harcourt Achieve.

———. 2007. *Nonfiction Readers Theatre for Beginning Readers.* Westport, CT: Teacher Ideas Press.

———. 2008a. *MORE Frantic Frogs and Other Frankly Fractured Folktales for Readers Theatre.* Westport, CT: Teacher Ideas Press.

———. 2008b. *African Legends, Myths, and Folktales for Readers Theatre.* Westport, CT: Teacher Ideas Press.

Martinez, M., N. Roser, and S. Strecker. 1999. "I Never Thought I Could Be a Star": A Readers Theatre Ticket to Reading Fluency." *The Reading Teacher* 52: 326–334.

Meinbach, A. M., A. D. Fredericks, and L. Rothlein. 2000. *The Complete Guide to Thematic Units: Creating the Integrated Curriculum.* Norwood, MA: Christopher-Gordon Publishers.

Rasinski, T. V. 2003. *The Fluent Reader: Oral Reading Strategies for Building Word Recognition, Fluency, and Comprehension.* New York: Scholastic.

Strecker, S. K., N. L. Roser, and M. G. Martinez. 1999. "Toward Understanding Oral Reading Fluency." *Yearbook of the National Reading Conference* 48: 295–310.

Tyler, B., and D. J. Chard. 2000. "Using Readers Theatre to Foster Fluency in Struggling Readers: A Twist on the Repeated Reading Strategy." *Reading and Writing Quarterly* 16: 163–168.

Wiggens, G., and J. McTighe. 1998. *Understanding by Design.* Alexandria, VA: Association for Supervision and Curriculum Development.

Wiske, M. S., ed. 1998. *Teaching for Understanding.* San Francisco: Jossey-Bass.

Wolf, S. 1998. "The Flight of Reading: Shifts in Instruction, Orchestration, and Attitudes Through Classroom Theatre." *Reading Research Quarterly* 33: 382–415.

More Teacher Resources

by

Anthony D. Fredericks

The following books are available from Teacher Ideas Press (130 Cremona Drive, Santa Barbara, CA 93117); 1-800-368-6868; http://www.teacherideaspress.com.

African Legends, Myths, and Folktales for Readers Theatre. ISBN 978-1-59158-633-3. (166pp.; $25.00).

Teachers are continually looking for materials that will enhance the study of cultures around the world. This collection of readers theatre scripts offers just that through an approach to the cultural study of Africa that will be fun and motivational for students—and improve their reading fluency.

Building Fluency with Readers Theatre: Motivational Strategies, Successful Lessons and Dynamic Scripts to Develop Fluency, Comprehension, Writing, and Vocabulary. ISBN 978-1-59158-733-0. (225pp.; $35.00).

Packed with practical ideas and loads of creative strategies, this resource offers teachers and librarians a wealth of innovative and dynamic techniques to stimulate and support the teaching of reading fluency across the elementary curriculum. This book is filled with the latest information, up-to-date data, and lots of inventive scripts for any classroom or library.

Frantic Frogs and Other Frankly Fractured Folktales for Readers Theatre. ISBN 1-56308-174-1. (123pp.; $19.50).

Have you heard "Don't Kiss Sleeping Beauty, She's Got Really Bad Breath" or "The Brussels Sprouts Man (The Gingerbread Man's Unbelievably Strange Cousin)"? This resource (grades 4–8) offers 30 reproducible satirical scripts for rip-roaring dramatics in any classroom or library.

The Integrated Curriculum: Books for Reluctant Readers, Grades 2–5 (2nd Edition). ISBN 0-87287-994-1. (220pp.; $22.50).

This book presents guidelines for motivating and using literature with reluctant readers. The book contains more than 40 book units on titles carefully selected to motivate the most reluctant readers.

Investigating Natural Disasters Through Children's Literature: An Integrated Approach. ISBN 1-56308-861-4. (193pp.; $28.00).

Tap into students' inherent awe of storms, volcanic eruptions, hurricanes, earthquakes, tornadoes, floods, avalanches, landslides, and tsunamis to open their minds to the wonders and power of the natural world.

Involving Parents Through Children's Literature: P–K. ISBN 1-56308-022-2. (86pp.; $15.00).

Involving Parents Through Children's Literature: Grades 1–2. ISBN 1-56308-012-5. (95pp.; $14.50).

Involving Parents Through Children's Literature: Grades 3–4. ISBN 1-56308-013-3. (96pp.; $15.50).

Involving Parents Through Children's Literature: Grades 5–6. ISBN 1-56308-014-1. (107pp.; $16.00)

This series of four books offers engaging activities for adults and children that stimulate comprehension and promote reading enjoyment. Reproducible activity sheets based on high-quality children's books are designed in a convenient format so that children can take them home.

The Librarian's Complete Guide to Involving Parents Through Children's Literature: Grades K–6. ISBN 1-56308-538-0. (137pp.; $24.50).

Activities for 101 children's books are presented in a reproducible format, so librarians can distribute them to students to take home and share with parents.

MORE Frantic Frogs and Other Frankly Fractured Folktales for Readers Theatre. ISBN 978-1-59158-628-9. (154pp.; $25.00).

Remember all the fun you had with the original *Frantic Frogs*? Well, they're back!! Here's another laugh-fest overflowing with scripts that will leave students (and teachers) rolling in the aisles. (Don't miss "The Original Hip-Hop [by Busta Frog]".)

MORE Science Adventures with Children's Literature: Reading Comprehension and Inquiry-Based Science. ISBN 978-1-59158-619-7. (443pp.; $35.00).

Get ready for hundreds of hands-on, minds-on projects that will actively engage students in positive learning experiences. Each of the 62 units offers book summaries, science topic areas, critical thinking questions, classroom resources, reproducible pages, and lots of easy-to-do activities, including science experiments for every grade level.

MORE Social Studies Through Children's Literature: An Integrated Approach. ISBN 1-56308-761-8. (225pp.; $27.50).

Energize your social studies curriculum with dynamic, hands-on, minds-on projects based on such great children's books as *Amazing Grace*, *Fly Away Home*, and *Lon Po Po*. This books is filled with an array of activities and projects sure to "energize" any social studies curriculum.

Mother Goose Readers Theatre for Beginning Readers. ISBN 978-1-59158-500-8. (168pp.; $25.00).

Designed especially for educators in the primary grades, this resource provides engaging opportunities that capitalize on children's enjoyment of Mother Goose rhymes. There lots to share and lots to enjoy in the pages of this resource.

MUCH MORE Social Studies Through Children's Literature: A Collaborative Approach. ISBN 978-1-59158-445-2. (256pp.; $35.00).

This collection of dynamic literature-based activities will help any teacher or librarian energize the entire social studies curriculum and implement national (and state) standards. This resource is filled with hundreds of hands-on, minds-on projects.

Nonfiction Readers Theatre for Beginning Readers. ISBN 978-1-59158-499-5. (220pp.; $25.00).

This collection of science and social studies nonfiction scripts for beginning readers is sure to "jazz up" any language arts program in grades 1–3. Teachers and librarians will discover a wealth of creative opportunities to enhance fluency, comprehension, and appreciation of nonfiction literature.

Readers Theatre for American History. ISBN 1-56308-860-6. (173pp.; $30.00).

This book offers a participatory approach to American history in which students become active participants in several historical events. These 24 scripts give students a "you are there" perspective on critical milestones and colorful moments that have shaped the American experience.

Science Adventures with Children's Literature: A Thematic Approach. ISBN 1-56308-417-1. (190pp.; $24.50).

Focusing on the National Science Education Standards, this activity-centered resource uses a wide variety of children's literature to integrate science across the elementary curriculum. With a thematic approach, it features the best in science trade books along with stimulating hands-on, minds on activities in all the sciences.

Science Discoveries on the Net: An Integrated Approach. ISBN 1-56308-823-1. (315pp.; $27.50).

This book is designed to help teachers integrate the Internet into their science programs and enhance the scientific discoveries of students. The 88 units emphasize key concepts—based on national and state standards—throughout the science curriculum.

Silly Salamanders and Other Slightly Stupid Stuff for Readers Theatre. ISBN 1-56308-825-8. (161pp.; $23.50).

The third entry in the "wild and wacky" readers theatre trilogy is just as crazy and just as weird as the first two. This unbelievable resource offers students in grades 3–6 dozens of silly send-ups of well-known fairy tales, legends, and original stories.

Social Studies Discoveries on the Net: An Integrated Approach. ISBN 1-56308-824-X. (276pp.; $26.00).

This book is designed to help teachers integrate the Internet into their social studies programs and enhance the classroom discoveries of students. The 75 units emphasize key concepts—based on national and state standards—throughout the social studies curriculum.

Social Studies Through Children's Literature: An Integrated Approach. ISBN 1-87287-970-4 (192pp.; $24.00).

Each of the 32 instructional units contained in this resource utilizes an activity-centered approach to elementary social studies, featuring children's picture books such as *Ox-Cart Man, In Coal Country,* and *Jambo Means Hello.*

Songs and Rhymes Readers Theatre for Beginning Readers. ISBN 978-1-59158-627-2. (154pp.; $25.00).

Bring music, song, and dance into your classroom language arts curriculum with this delightful collection of popular rhymes and ditties. Beginning readers will enjoy learning about familiar characters in this engaging collection of scripts.

Tadpole Tales and Other Totally Terrific Titles for Readers Theatr*e.* ISBN 1-56308-547-X. (115pp.; $18.50).

A follow-up volume to the best-selling *Frantic Frogs and Other Frankly Fractured Folktales for Readers Theatre,* this book provides primary level readers (grades 1–4) with a humorous assortment of wacky tales based on well-known Mother Goose rhymes. More than 30 scripts and dozens of extensions will keep students rolling in the aisles.

Index

Allington, R. L., xi
Audience. *See* Readers theatre performances: audience

"Beauty and the Beast," 17–21
"Beauty and This Incredibly Ugly Guy," 107–10

Chard, D. J., ix
"Chicken Little," 71–76
Children's literature and readers theatre, x
Choral reading, 6
"Cinderella," 99–104
Comprehension
    development, x
"Coughy: The Dwarf Snow White Never Told You About," 111–15
Cunningham, P., xi

Dixon, N. A., viii
"Don't Kiss Sleeping Beauty, She's Got Really Bad Breath," 116–18

"Elves and the Shoemaker, The," 22–25
"Emperor's New Clothes, The," 26–31
English/language arts standards, x, xi–xii

Fairy tales
    humorous, scripts for, 107–28
    and readers theatre, vii–viii
    readers theatre scripts for, 17–130
Frantic Frogs and Other Frankly Fractured Folktales for Readers Theatre, 3
Fredericks, A. D., viii, ix, 7

"Gingerbread Boy Gets Baked at 350° for 15–20 Minutes, The," 127–30
"Gingerbread Man, The," 62–66
"Goldilocks and the Three Bears," 67–70
"Goldilocks and the Three Hamsters," 119–22

"Hansel and Gretel," 32–35

IRA/NCTE Standards for the English Language Arts, xi–xii

"Jack and the Beanstalk," 36–40

Language arts and readers theatre, x
Literacy growth, impact of readers theatre on, viii–ix
"Little Red Hen, The," 59–61
"Little Red Riding Hood," 77–80
"Little Red Riding Hood Punches the Wolf Character Right in the Kisser," 123–26

Martinez, M., viii
McTighe, J., x
Meinbach, A. M., 7

"Princess and the Pea, The," 41–43

"Rapunzel," 44–48
Rasinski, Tim, viii
Readers theatre. *See also* Readers theatre scripts
    in classroom, 3–7
    and elements of children's literature, x
    and developing reading fluency, ix
    educational value of, ix
    effects on comprehension development, x
    and fairy tales, vii–viii
    familiarization with, 4, 5–6
    impact on literacy growth, viii–ix
    integration of, 4, 7
    introducing, 3–7
    performing. *See* Readers theatre performances
    in library, 3–7
    practice of, 4, 6–7
    research on impact of, viii–ix
    and standards, xi–xii
    value of, ix–xi
Readers theatre performances
    audience, 12–14
    delivery, 12
    post-presentation, 14
    presentation options, 13
    props, 11
    script preparation, 9–10
    script selection, 12
    staging, 10–11
    starting, 10

Readers theatre scripts
  "Beauty and the Beast," 17–21
  "Beauty and This Incredibly Ugly Guy," 107–10
  "Chicken Little," 71–76
  "Cinderella," 99–104
  "Coughy: The Dwarf Snow White Never Told You About," 111–15
  "Don't Kiss Sleeping Beauty, She's Got Really Bad Breath," 116–18
  "The Elves and the Shoemaker," 22–25
  "The Emperor's New Clothes," 26–31
  "The Gingerbread Boy Gets Baked at 350° for 15–20 Minutes," 127–30
  "The Gingerbread Man," 62–66
  "Goldilocks and the Three Bears," 67–70
  "Goldilocks and the Three Hamsters," 119–22
  "Hansel and Gretel," 32–35
  "Jack and the Beanstalk," 36–40
  "The Little Red Hen," 59–61
  "Little Red Riding Hood," 77–80
  "Little Red Riding Hood Punches the Wolf Character Right in the Kisser," 123–26
  "The Princess and the Pea," 41–43
  "Rapunzel," 44–48
  "Rumpelstiltskin," 49–53
  "Sleeping Beauty," 94–98
  "Snow White and the Seven Dwarfs," 54–58
  "The Three Billy Goats Gruff," 90–93
  "The Three Little Pigs," 81–84
  "The Ugly Duckling," 85–89
"Rumpelstiltskin," 49–53

Sentence strips, 5, 6
"Sleeping Beauty," 94–98. *See also* "Don't Kiss Sleeping Beauty, She's Got Really Bad Breath"
"Snow White and the Seven Dwarfs," 54–58
Stages for introducing readers theatre, 3–7
Standards. *See* English/language arts standards
Strecker, S. K., ix

"Three Billy Goats Gruff, The," 90–93
"Three Little Pigs, The," 81–84
Tyler, B., ix

"Ugly Duckling, The," 85–89

Wiggens, G., x
Wiske, M. S., x
Wolf, S., viii

About the Author

Anthony D. Fredericks (afredericks60@comcast.net). Tony's background includes more than 39 years of experience as a classroom teacher, reading specialist, curriculum coordinator, staff developer, professional storyteller, and college professor. He is a prolific author, having written more than 75 teacher resource books, including the enormously popular *MORE Frantic Frogs and Other Frankly Fractured Folktales for Readers Theatre,* the best-selling *Building Fluency with Readers Theatre,* the celebrated *MUCH MORE Social Studies Through Children's Literature*, and the dynamic *Readers Theatre for American History.*

In addition, he has authored more than three dozen award-winning children's books, including *The Tsunami Quilt: Grandfather's Story*; *Near One Cattail: Turtles, Logs and Leaping Frogs*; *Dinosaur Droppings, Animal Sharpshooters*; and *A Is for Anaconda: A Rainforest Alphabet Book.*

Tony currently teaches elementary methods courses in reading, language arts, science, social studies, and children's literature at York College in York, Pennsylvania. In addition, he is a popular and enthusiastic visiting children's author to elementary schools throughout North America, where he celebrates books, writing, and storytelling.